The Phantom of the Opera

THE PHANTOM OF THE OPERA

Gaston Leroux

Edited and abridged by Doris Dickens

Illustrations by Wayne Anderson

ARMADA

First published in 1911
This illustrated edition first published
in Armada in 1988
This impression 1989

Armada is an imprint of
the Children's Division, part of
the Collins Publishing Group,
8 Grafton Street, London W1X 3LA

Printed and bound in Great Britain by
William Collins Sons & Co. Ltd, Glasgow

Introduction

Having seen a classic work of literature performed on television, on the stage or at a cinema, children are often disappointed and frustrated when they cannot read and understand the original work. With this in mind, Doris Dickens, great-granddaughter of Charles Dickens and a former teacher, has edited and abridged many well-known books including *Oliver Twist*, *The Old Curiosity Shop*, *The Children of the New Forest*, *Little Men*, *Dracula*, *Lorna Doone* and now *The Phantom of the Opera*.

Contents

CHAPTER I

Is it The Ghost?

It was the evening on which Monsieur Debienne and Monsieur Poligny, the managers of the Opera, were giving a farewell gala performance to mark their retirement. Suddenly, the dressing room of La Sorelli, one of the principal dancers, was invaded by half a dozen young ladies of the ballet, who had just come off stage. They rushed in amid great confusion, some giving way to hysterical laughter, others to cries of terror. Sorelli, who wanted to be alone for a moment to polish up the speech which she was to make in honour of the resigning managers, looked round angrily at the mad and tumultuous crowd. It was little Jammes – the girl with the tip-tilted nose, the forget-me-not eyes, the rose-red cheeks and the lily-white neck and shoulders – who gave the explanation in a trembling voice:

"It's the ghost!"

And she locked the door.

Sorelli's dressing room was elegant. It had a pier-glass,

a sofa, a dressing table and a cupboard or two, and these provided the necessary furniture. On the walls hung a few engravings which had belonged to Sorelli's mother, who was herself a famous dancer.

The room seemed a palace to the girls of the *corps de ballet*, who were lodged in common dressing rooms where they spent their time singing, quarrelling, smacking the dressers and hairdressers and buying one another drinks until the callboy's bell rang.

Sorelli was very superstitious. She shuddered when she heard little Jammes speak of the ghost, called her a silly little fool and then at once asked for details:

"Have you seen him?"

"As plainly as I see you now!" moaned Jammes, whose legs were giving way beneath her, and she dropped into a chair.

Thereupon Giry – the girl with eyes black as sloes, hair black as ink, a swarthy complexion and a poor little skin stretched over poor little bones – added:

"If that's the ghost, he's very ugly!"

"Oh yes!" cried the chorus of ballet girls.

And they all began to talk together. The ghost had appeared to them in the shape of a gentleman in dress clothes, who had suddenly stood before them in the passage, without their knowing where he came from. He seemed to have loomed through the wall.

"Pooh!" said one of them who had more or less kept her head. "You see the ghost everywhere!"

And it was true. For several months there had been nothing discussed at the Opera but this ghost in dress clothes, who stalked about the building, from top to bottom, like a shadow, who spoke to nobody, to whom nobody dared to speak and who vanished as soon as he was seen, no one knowing how or where. All the girls pretended to have met him and all mishaps, comic or serious, were put down to him. Had anyone met with a fall, or suffered a practical joke at the hands of one of the other girls, or lost a powder puff, it was the fault of the Opera Ghost.

Yet who had actually seen him? You meet so many men in dress clothes at the Opera who are not ghosts. But this dress suit had a peculiarity of its own: it clothed a skeleton. At least, so the ballet girls said. And, of course, it had a death's head.

Was all this serious? The truth is that the idea of the skeleton came from the description of the ghost given by Joseph Buquet, the chief scene-shifter, who had really seen the ghost. He had run up against the ghost on the little staircase, by the footlights, which leads straight down to the cellars. He had seen him for a second – for the ghost had fled – and to anyone who cared to listen to him he said:

"He is extraordinarily thin and his dress coat hangs on a skeleton frame. His eyes are so deep that you can hardly see the fixed pupils. All you see is two big black holes, as in a dead man's skull. His skin, which is stretched across his bones like a drumhead, is not white, but a dirty yellow. His nose is so little worth talking about that you can't see it side-face; and *the absence* of that nose is a horrible thing *to look at*. All the hair he has is three or four long dark locks on his forehead and behind the ears."

Joseph Buquet was a serious, sober, steady man, very slow at imagining things. Some people said that they too had met a man in dress clothes with a death's head on his shoulders. Others thought he had been the victim of a joke played by one of his assistants. And then, one after the other, such curious things happened that the very shrewdest people began to feel uneasy.

For instance, a fireman is a brave fellow! He fears nothing, least of all fire! Well, a fireman who was called Pampin had gone to make a round of inspection in the cellars and seems to have ventured a little further than usual. Suddenly he reappeared on the stage, pale, scared, and trembling, with his eyes starting out of his head, and practically fainted in the arms of the proud mother of little Jammes. And why? Because he had seen, coming towards him, *at the level of his head, but without a body attached to it, a head of fire!* And, as I said, a fireman is not afraid of fire.

The *corps de ballet* was flung into consternation. At first sight this fiery head in no way matched Joseph Buquet's description of the ghost. But the young ladies soon persuaded themselves that the ghost had several heads, which he changed about as he pleased. And, of course, they at once imagined that they were in the greatest danger and walked quickly past dark corners and through badly-lit corridors.

That same evening the girls were in their dressing room and Sorelli was with them. Suddenly little Jammes cried out, "It's the ghost!" There was an agonizing silence; nothing was heard but the hard breathing of the girls. At last Jammes, flinging herself into the furthest corner of the wall, with every mark of real terror on her face, whispered, "Listen!" Everybody seemed to hear a rustling outside the door. There was no sound of footsteps. It was like light silk gliding along the panel. Then it stopped.

Sorelli tried to show more pluck than the others. She went up to the door and, in a quavering voice, asked, "Who's there?"

But nobody answered. Then, feeling all eyes upon her, she made an effort to show courage and said, very loudly, "Is there anyone behind the door?"

"Oh yes, there is! Of course there is!" cried that little dried plum of a Meg Giry, heroically holding Sorelli back by her gauze skirt. "Whatever you do, don't open the door! Oh lord, don't open the door!"

But Sorelli, armed with a dagger which she always carried, turned the key and drew back the door, while the ballet girls retreated to the inner dressing room and Meg Giry moaned, "Mother! Mother!"

Sorelli looked into the passage bravely. It was empty. A gas flame, in its glass prison, cast a red and sinister light into the surrounding darkness, but she could see little, and the dancer slammed the door again, with a deep sigh.

"No," she said, "there is no one there."

Sorelli looked at the frightened girls and added, "Come, children, pull yourselves together! I daresay no one has ever seen the ghost . . ."

"Yes, yes, we saw him . . . we saw him just now!" cried the girls. "He had his death's head and his dress coat, just as when he appeared to Joseph Buquet!"

"And Gabriel saw him too!" said Jammes, "Only yesterday! Yesterday afternoon . . . in broad daylight."

"Gabriel, the chorus-master?"

"Why yes, didn't you know?"

"And he was wearing his dress clothes, in broad daylight?"

"Who? Gabriel?"

"Why no, the ghost!"

"Certainly! Gabriel told me so himself. That's what he knew him by. Gabriel was in the stage-manager's office. Suddenly the door opened and the Persian entered. You know, the Persian has the evil eye . . ."

"Oh yes!" answered the little ballet girls in chorus, warding off bad luck by pointing their forefinger and little finger at the absent Persian, while their second and third fingers were bent on the palm and held down by the thumb.

"And you know how superstitious Gabriel is," continued Jammes. "However, he is always polite, and, when he meets the Persian, he just puts his hand in his pocket and touches his keys. Well, the moment the Persian appeared in the doorway, Gabriel gave one jump from his chair to the lock of the cupboard, so as to touch iron! In so doing, he tore the sleeve of his coat on a nail. Hurrying to get out of the room, he banged his forehead against a hatpeg and gave himself a huge bump; then, suddenly stepping back, he skinned his arm on the screen, near the piano. He tried to lean on the piano, but the lid fell on his

13

hands and crushed his fingers. He rushed out of the office like a madman, slipped on the staircase and came down the whole of the first flight on his back. I was just passing with Mother. We picked him up. He was covered with bruises and his face was all over blood. We were frightened out of our lives, but, all at once, he began to thank Providence that he had got off so cheaply. Then he told us what had frightened him. He had seen the ghost behind the Persian, *the ghost with the death's head*, just like Joseph Buquet's description!"

Jammes had told her story ever so quickly, as though the ghost were at her heels, and was quite out of breath at the finish.

A silence followed, while Sorelli polished her nails in great excitement. It was broken by little Giry, who said, "Joseph Buquet would do better to hold his tongue."

"Why should he hold his tongue?" asked somebody.

"That's Ma's opinion," replied Meg, lowering her voice and looking about her, as though fearing she might be heard outside the room.

"And why is it your mother's opinion?"

"Hush! Ma says the ghost doesn't like being talked about. I mustn't say any more. I swore not to tell," gasped Meg.

But the girls left her no peace and promised to keep the secret, until Meg, burning to say all she knew, began, with her eyes fixed on the door:

"Well, it's because of the private box . . ."

"What private box?"

"The ghost's box!"

"Has the ghost a box? Oh, do tell us, do tell us! . . ."

"Not so loud," said Meg. "It's Box Five, you know, the box on the grand tier, next to the stage-box, on the left."

"Oh nonsense!"

"I tell you it is . . . Ma has charge of it . . . But you swear you won't say a word?"

"Of course, of course . . ."

"Well, that's the ghost's box, and orders have been given at the box office that it must never be sold . . ."

"And does the ghost really come there?"

"Yes . . ."

"Then somebody does come?"

"Why, no . . . The ghost comes, but there is nobody there."

The little ballet girls exchanged glances. If the ghost came to the box, he must be seen, because he wore a dress coat and a death's head. This was what they tried to make Meg understand, but she replied, "That's just it! The ghost is not seen. And he has no dress coat and no head! All that talk about his death's head and his head of fire is nonsense! There's nothing in it . . . You only *hear* him, when he is in the box. Ma has never seen him, but she has heard him. Ma knows, because she gives him his programme."

Sorelli interfered: "Giry, child, you're having us on!"

Little Giry began to cry. "I ought to have held my tongue . . . If Ma ever got to know! But it's true enough, Joseph Buquet had no business to talk of things that don't concern him . . . it will bring him bad luck. Ma was saying so last night."

There was a sound of heavy and hurried footsteps in the passage, and a breathless voice cried, "Cécile! Cécile! Are you there?"

"It's my Ma's voice," said Jammes. "What's the matter?"

She opened the door. A respectable lady, built on the lines of a Grenadier Guard, burst into the dressing room, and dropped groaning into a vacant armchair.

"How awful!" she cried. "How awful!"

"What? What? . . ."

"Joseph Buquet . . ."

"What about him?"

"Joseph Buquet is dead."

The room became filled with exclamations, with astonished outcries, with scared requests for explanations . . .

15

"Yes, he was found hanging in the third-floor cellar!"

"It's the ghost," blurted out little Giry, and all around her the girls repeated under their breaths, "Yes, it must be the ghost."

Sorelli was very pale.

"I shall never be able to recite my speech," she said.

Ma Jammes gave her opinion, while she drained a glass of brandy which happened to be standing on the table: "The ghost must have had something to do with it."

Joseph Buquet's body had been found hanging from a rope in the third cellar under the stage by Mercier, the acting manager. He rushed for helpers to cut him down, but, when he returned, both man and rope had disappeared.

The horrid news soon spread all over the Opera, where Joseph Buquet was very popular. The dressing rooms emptied and the little ballet girls, crowding round Sorelli like timid sheep around their shepherdess, made for the foyer through the ill-lit passages and staircases, trotting as fast as their little pink legs could carry them.

CHAPTER II

The New Margarita

On the first landing, Sorelli ran against the Comte de Chagny, who was coming upstairs. The count, who was generally so calm, seemed greatly excited.

"I was just coming to you," he said, taking off his hat. "Oh, Sorelli, what an evening! And Christine Daaé: what a triumph!"

"Impossible!" said Meg Giry. "Six months ago, she sang like a carrion crow! But do let us get by, my dear count," she continued with a cheeky curtsey. "We are going to enquire after a poor man who has been found hanging by the neck."

Just then, the acting-manager came fussing past and stopped when he heard this remark.

"What!" he exclaimed roughly. "Have you girls already heard about it? Well, please forget about it for tonight. We don't want to upset the retiring managers on their last day."

They all went down to the foyer, which was already full of people. The Comte de Chagny was right. No gala performance had ever equalled this. All the great composers of the day had conducted their own works in turn, well-known singers had performed and, on that evening, Christine Daaé had revealed her true self. Hers was the real triumph. She had begun by singing a few passages from *Romeo and Juliet*. This was the first time the young artiste had sung in this work of Gounod, and those who heard her say that her voice was seraphic, but this was nothing to her singing in the prison scene and the final trio in *Faust*, which she sang in the place of the star Carlotta, who was ill. No one had ever seen or heard anything like it.

The whole house went mad, rising to its feet, shouting, cheering, clapping, while Christine sobbed and fainted in the arms of her fellow singers and had to be carried to her dressing-room. A few subscribers, however, protested. Why had so great a treasure been kept from them all that time? If Carlotta had not been absent, Christine would never have had a chance to show what she could do. Why had she kept her talent hidden for so long? She was not known to have a professor of singing at that time and she often said that she meant to practise by herself in future. The whole thing was a mystery.

The Comte de Chagny, standing up in his box, listened to all this frenzy and took part in it by loudly applauding. Philippe de Chagny was just forty-one years of age. He was a great aristocrat and a good-looking man, tall and with attractive features, in spite of his hard forehead and his rather cold eyes. At the death of his father, he had taken charge of his young brother Raoul since their mother, the Comtesse, had died giving birth to Raoul who was twenty years younger than Philippe. Philippe put Raoul into the navy; he had finished his training and was now on leave and at the Opera with his brother. Raoul was twenty-one and looked eighteen. He had a small fair moustache, beautiful blue eyes, a complexion like a girl's and considerable charm.

On that evening, Philippe, after applauding Christine, turned to his brother and saw that he was quite pale.

"Don't you see," said Raoul, "that the woman is fainting?"

"You look like fainting yourself," said the count. "What's the matter?"

But Raoul had recovered himself and was standing up.

"Let's go," he said, in a trembling voice.

"Where do you want to go to, Raoul?" asked the count, astonished at the excitement shown by his younger brother.

"Let's go and see her. She never sang like that before."

The count gave his brother a curious, smiling glance and seemed quite pleased. They were soon at the door leading from the house to the stage. Numbers of subscribers were slowly passing through. Raoul tore his gloves without knowing what he was doing, and Philippe had much too kind a heart to laugh at him for his impatience. But he now understood why Raoul was absent-minded when spoken to and why he always tried to turn every conversation to the subject of the Opera.

They pushed their way through the crowds until they came to a dark corridor ringing with the name of "Daaé! Daaé!" The count was surprised to find that Raoul knew the way. He had never taken him to Christine's room himself and he came to the conclusion that Raoul must have gone there alone while the count stayed talking in the foyer with Sorelli, who often asked him to wait until it was her time to go on stage.

Postponing his usual visit to Sorelli for a few minutes, the count followed his brother down the passage that led to Christine's dressing room and saw it had never been so crammed as on that evening, when the whole house seemed excited by her success and also by her fainting fit.

19

For Christine had not yet recovered consciousness and the theatre doctor had just arrived. So it happened that Christine received first aid from him while opening her eyes in the arms of Raoul.

"Don't you think, doctor, that these people had better clear the room?" asked Raoul coolly. "There's no breathing here."

"You are quite right," said the doctor.

And he sent every one away, except Raoul and the maid, who looked at Raoul with eyes of astonishment. She had never seen him before and yet dared not question him, and the doctor imagined that the young man was acting as he did because he had every right to. Raoul, therefore, remained in the room and watched Christine slowly recover while the Comte de Chagny went outside with the others. "My brother is a dark horse," he said to himself, chuckling, and he went away to visit Sorelli.

Christine Daaé opened her eyes and looked at Raoul.

"Monsieur," she said, in a voice not much above a whisper, "who are you?"

"Mademoiselle," replied the young man, kneeling on one knee and pressing a fervent kiss on Christine's hand, *"I am the little boy who went into the sea to rescue your scarf."*

Christine looked at the doctor and the maid, and all three began to laugh.

Raoul turned very red and stood up.

"Mademoiselle," he said. "Since you are pleased not to recognize me, I should like to say something to you in private, something very important."

"When I am better, do you mind?" And her voice shook. "You have been very kind."

"Yes, you must go," said the doctor, with his most pleasant smile. "Leave me to attend to Mademoiselle."

"I am not ill now," said Christine, suddenly, with strange and unexpected energy.

She rose and, passing her hand over her eyes, said, "Thank you, doctor . . . I should like to be alone . . .

Please go away, all of you . . . Leave me . . . I feel very restless this evening . . ."

The doctor, seeing her agitation, thought it best not to upset her further, and he went away, saying to Raoul who followed him outside, "She is not herself tonight . . . She is usually so gentle . . ."

Then he said good night, and Raoul was left alone. The whole of this part of the theatre was now deserted. Raoul supposed the farewell party for the retiring managers Debienne and Poligny must be taking place in the foyer. He thought that Christine might go to it, and he waited in the silent solitude, even hid himself in the kindly shadow of a doorway. He still felt a terrible pain at his heart, and it was of this that he wished to speak to Christine without delay. Suddenly the dressing room door opened and the maid came out by herself, carrying bundles. He stopped her and asked how her mistress was. The woman laughed and said that she was quite well, but that he must not disturb her, for she wished to be left alone. And the maid went away. A single idea crossed Raoul's burning brain: of course, Christine wished to be alone *for him*! Had he not told her that he wanted to speak to her privately?

Hardly breathing, he went up to the dressing room and, with his ear to the door to catch her reply, prepared to knock. But his hand dropped. He had heard a *man's voice* in the dressing room, saying, in a curiously masterful tone, "Christine, you must love me!" And Christine's voice, infinitely sad and trembling, as though accompanied by tears, replied, "How can you talk like that? *When I sing only for you?* . . ."

The man's voice spoke again:

"Are you very tired?"

"Oh, tonight, I gave you my soul and I am dead!"

"Your soul is a beautiful thing, child," replied the man's grave voice, "and I thank you. No emperor ever received so fair a gift. *The angels wept tonight.*"

Raoul heard nothing after that. Nevertheless he did not

21

go away but returned to his dark corner, determined to wait for the man to leave the room. At one and the same time, he had learnt what love meant – and hatred. He knew that he loved. He wanted to know whom he hated. To his great astonishment, the door opened and Christine Daaé appeared, wrapped in furs, with her face hidden in a lace veil, alone. She closed the door behind her, but Raoul observed that she did not lock it. She passed him. He did not even follow her with his eyes, for his eyes were fixed on the door, which did not open again.

When the passage was once more deserted, he crossed it, opened the door of the dressing room, went in and shut the door. He found himself in absolute darkness. The gas had been turned out.

"There is someone here!" said Raoul, with his back against the closed door, in a quivering voice. "What are you hiding for?"

All was darkness and silence. Raoul heard only the sound of his own breathing. "You shan't leave this room until I let you!" he exclaimed. "If you don't answer, you are a coward! But I'll show you up!"

And he struck a match. Its flame lit the room. There was no one in the room! Raoul, first turning the key in the door, lit the gas-jets. He went into the dressing closet, opened the cupboards, hunted about, felt the walls with his moist hands. Nothing!

"Look here!" he said, aloud. "Am I going mad?"

He stood for ten minutes listening to the gas flaring in the silence of the empty room, and then went out, not knowing what he was doing nor where he was going. Suddenly an icy draught struck him in the face. He found himself at the foot of a staircase down which, behind him, a procession of workmen were carrying a sort of stretcher, covered with a white sheet.

"Which is the way out, please?" he asked one of the men.

"Straight in front of you. The door is open. Please let us pass."

Pointing to the stretcher, he asked, mechanically:

"What is that?"

The workman answered:

"'That' is Joseph Buquet, who was found hanging in the third cellar."

Raoul took off his hat, fell back to make way for the procession and went out.

CHAPTER III

Why the Managers Resigned

During this time, the farewell ceremony for the retiring managers was taking place. The social and artistic world of Paris was assembled in the foyer where Sorelli waited with a glass of champagne in her hand and a little prepared speech at the tip of her tongue. Behind her, the members of the *corps de ballet*, young and old, discussed the events of the day in whispers, or exchanged little waves with their friends, a noisy crowd who surrounded the supper tables arranged along the slanting floor.

A few of the dancers had already changed into ordinary dress, but most of them still wore their skirts of gossamer gauze, and all had thought it the right thing to put on a special face for the occasion: all, that is, except little Jammes, whose fifteen summers seemed already to have forgotten the ghost and the death of Joseph Buquet. She never ceased to laugh and chatter, to hop about and play practical jokes until Monsieur Debienne and Monsieur Poligny appeared on the steps of the foyer, when she was severely called to order by the impatient Sorelli.

The managers were trying rather too hard to look cheerful and Sorelli had begun to recite her speech, when an exclamation from little Jammes wiped the smile off their faces so brutally that the expression of distress and dismay that lay beneath it became obvious to all eyes.

"The Opera Ghost!"

Jammes yelled these words in a tone of unspeakable terror and her finger pointed, among the crowd of dandies, to a face so pale, so mournful and so ugly, with two such deep black holes under the straddling eyebrows, that the death's-head in question immediately scored a huge success.

"The Opera Ghost! The Opera Ghost!"

Everybody laughed and pushed his neighbour and wanted to offer the Opera Ghost a drink; but he was gone. He had slipped through the crowd, and the others vainly hunted for him, while two old gentlemen tried to calm little Jammes and while little Giry stood screeching like a peacock.

Sorelli was furious. She had not been able to finish her speech; the managers had kissed her, thanked her and run away as fast as the ghost himself. No one was surprised at this, for it was known that they were to go through the same ceremony on the floor above, in the foyer of the singers, and that finally they were themselves to receive their personal friends, for the last time, in the great lobby outside the managers' office, where a sit-down supper would be served.

Here they met the new managers Monsieur Armand Montcharmin and Monsieur Firmin Richard, whom they hardly knew; nevertheless they made lavish assurances of friendship and received a thousand flattering compliments in reply. The supper was quite jolly, and even those who were there from a sense of duty enjoyed themselves.

The retiring managers had already handed over to their successors the two little master-keys which opened all the doors – thousands of doors – of the Opera House. And those tiny keys, the object of general curiosity, were being passed from hand to hand when the attention of some of the guests was drawn away by the discovery, at the end of the table, of that strange, wan, fantastic face, with hollow eyes, which had already appeared in the foyer of the ballet and been greeted by little Jammes's exclamation:

"The Opera Ghost!"

There sat the ghost as natural as could be, except that he neither ate nor drank. Those who began by looking at him with a smile ended by turning away their heads, for the sight of him at once brought on the most deathly thoughts. No one repeated the joke of the foyer, no one exclaimed: "There's the Opera Ghost!"

He himself did not speak a word. The friends of the new managers thought that he had been invited by the old managers and their friends thought that he was a guest of Firmin Richard and Armand Montcharmin. The result was that no request was made for an explanation, no unpleasant remark, no joke in bad taste, which might have offended this visitor from the tomb.

The former managers who were sitting at the centre of the table had actually not seen the man with the death's head until suddenly he spoke:

"The dancers are right," he said. "The death of that poor Buquet is perhaps not as natural as people think."

Debienne and Poligny gave a start:

"Is Buquet dead?" they cried.

"Yes," replied the man, or the shadow of a man, quietly. "He was found this evening, hanging in the third cellar."

The two former managers at once rose and stared strangely at the speaker.

Then they looked at each other. They had both turned whiter than the tablecloth. At last, Debienne made a sign to Richard and Moncharmin; Poligny muttered a few words of excuse to the guests, and all four went into the managers' office.

The former managers appeared to have something difficult to tell their successors. At last they came out with it: they knew about the ghost, but would never have mentioned him if he had not given them formal orders to ask the new managers to be pleasant to him and to grant any request that he might make. They had put off doing this as long as they could, when the death of Joseph Buquet came as a brutal reminder that, whenever they paid no attention to the ghost's wishes, something fantastic or disastrous happened.

The new managers were inclined to take all this rather lightly and Richard asked, half seriously and half in jest:

"But, after all, what does this ghost of yours want?"

Monsieur Poligny went to his desk and returned with a copy of the Opera lease. This set out the conditions under which the Opera must be run and was naturally known to the new managers who had been given a copy. If the conditions were not met, the managers would no longer have the privilege of arranging the performances of the National Academy of Music of France. However, the office copy had a further clause written in red ink in rather childish writing which stated: "The privilege will also be withdrawn if the manager shall fail to pay the monthly allowance of 20,000 francs to the Opera Ghost."

Monsieur Poligny pointed with a shaking finger to this last clause which, of course, the new managers had not seen before. They were inclined to take it as a joke.

"Is this all? Doesn't he want anything more?" asked Richard, with the greatest coolness.

"Yes, he does," replied Poligny.

And he turned over the pages of the lease until he came to the clause which stated the days on which certain private boxes were to be reserved for the free use of the President of the Republic, the ministers and so on. At the end of the clause, a line had been added, also in red ink:

"Box Five on the grand tier shall be placed at the disposal of the Opera Ghost for every performance."

The new managers treated this as a joke as well and Richard said that he now understood why Monsieur Debienne and Monsieur Poligny were retiring from the management of the National Academy. Business was impossible with so unreasonable a ghost!

"You are quite right," said Poligny, without moving a muscle of his face. "We really can't work to keep ghosts! We prefer to go away."

"Yes," echoed Debienne, "we prefer to go away. Let us go."

And he stood up. Richard said:

"But, after all, it seems to me that you were very much too good to the ghost. If I had such a troublesome ghost as that, I should not hesitate to have him arrested . . ."

"But how? Where?" they cried, in chorus. "We have never seen him!"

"But when he comes to his box?"

"*We have never seen him in his box!*"

"Then sell it."

"Sell the Opera Ghost's box! Well, gentlemen, you try it!"

Thereupon they all four left the office. Richard and Montcharmin had never laughed so much in their lives.

CHAPTER IV

Box Five

The first few days which the new managers Armand Montcharmin and Firmin Richard spent at the Opera were given over to the delight of finding themselves the heads of so magnificent an enterprise, and they had forgotten all about the curious, fantastic story of the ghost, when something occurred which proved to them that the joke – if it *was* a joke, was not over. Mr Firmin Richard reached his office that morning at eleven o'clock. His secretary, Monsieur Rémy, showed him half a dozen letters which he had not opened because they were marked "private". One of the letters at once attracted Richard's attention, not only because the envelope was addressed in red ink, but because he seemed to recognize the clumsy, childish handwriting. He opened the letter and read:

Dear Mr Manager,
    I am sorry to have to trouble you when you must be so very busy at the moment. I should like to hear Christine Daaé sing tonight, and I must ask you not to sell Box Five (my box) today *nor on the following days*. For

I must tell you how disagreeably surprised I have been lately, on arriving at the Opera, to hear that my box had been sold, at the box office, by your orders. I did not protest at first because I thought that Monsieur Debienne and Monsieur Poligny had forgotten to tell you about my special clause in the lease. I wrote to ask them about it and received a reply in a theatrical newspaper that proves you know all about *my clause in the lease* and that therefore you are treating me with outrageous contempt. If you wish us to live in peace, you must not begin by taking away my private box.

Believe me to be, dear Mr Manager,

your most humble servant,

"Opera Ghost".

The letter was accompanied by a cutting from the personal column of *The Theatrical Revue*, which ran:

"O. G. – There is no excuse for R. and M. We told them about it and called their attention to your clause in the lease concerning Box Five. Kind regards."

Monsieur Firmin Richard had hardly finished reading this letter, when Monsieur Armand Montcharmin entered carrying one exactly like it. They looked at each other and burst out laughing:

"They are keeping up the joke," said Monsieur Richard, "but I don't call it funny."

"What does it all mean?" asked Monsieur Montcharmin. "Do they imagine that, because they have been managers of the Opera, we are going to let them have a box for their own use?"

"I am not in the mood to allow myself to be humbugged much longer," said Firmin Richard.

"It's harmless enough," observed Armand Montcharmin. "What is it they really want? A box for tonight?"

Monsieur Firmin Richard told his secretary to give Box Five on the grand tier to Monsieur Debienne and Monsieur Poligny, provided it was not already sold for that night. It

30

was not. The tickets were sent round to them. Debienne lived at the corner of the Rue Scribe and the Boulevard des Capucines; Poligny in the Rue Auber. O. Ghost's two letters had been posted at the Boulevard des Capucines post office, as Montcharmin remarked after examining the envelopes.

"You see!" said Richard, "they want the box for themselves."

They shrugged their shoulders and regretted that two men of that age should amuse themselves with such childish tricks. They dismissed the matter from their minds and Richard ordered the artistes to be shown in who, for the last two hours, had been walking up and down outside the door behind which fame and fortune – or dismissal – awaited them.

The whole day was spent in discussing, negotiating, signing or cancelling contracts; and the two over-worked managers went to bed early, without so much as casting a glance at Box Five to see whether Monsieur Debienne and Monsieur Poligny were enjoying the performance.

Next morning, the managers received a card of thanks from the ghost:

Dear Mr Manager,
 Thanks. Charming evening. Christine Daaé exquisite. Choruses want waking up. Carlotta rather common-place. Will write you soon for my annual allowance, less the 6575 francs 30 centimes paid me by the former managers for the ten days when they were in charge.
 Kind regards,
O. G.

There was also a letter from the former managers thanking Monsieur Firmin Richard for his kind thought, but saying they had no right to Box Five and that according to the special clause in the lease which he had seen, it was the exclusive property of the Opera Ghost.

31

"Those fellows are beginning to annoy me!" shouted Firmin Richard, snatching up the letter.

And that evening, Box Five was sold.

The next morning, when the managers reached their office, they found a report from an inspector concerning an incident that had happened the night before in Box Five. It seemed that the occupants, who had arrived as the curtain rose for the second act had been noisy, laughing and saying stupid things so that there were cries of "Hush" all round them and people were becoming extremely annoyed. The box-keeper had called the inspector who went to the box and asked the occupants to be quiet. They did not seem to be in their right minds and made silly remarks in answer to his request.

As soon as he left the box, the laughter started again and there were more protests from the audience, so he went back and turned the occupants out. When he was sent for, the inspector did not seem to be able to add to this story, so Monsieur Richard's secretary, Monsieur Rémy, sent for the box-keeper. She worked as a portress near the Opera and, soon after the inspector left, looking rather baffled, she made an appearance.

"What's your name?"

"Madame Giry. You know me well enough, sir; I am the mother of Meg, the dancer – little Giry as they call her."

This was said in so severe and solemn a tone, that, for a moment, Monsieur Richard was impressed. He looked at Madame Giry, in her faded shawl, her worn shoes, her old taffeta dress and dingy bonnet. It was obvious from his attitude that he either did not know or could not remember Mrs Giry or her daughter little Meg Giry, but Madame Giry was so proud of her daughter that she imagined everybody knew her.

"Never heard of her!" declared Monsieur Richard, "but I am hoping that you will be able to tell me what happened last night in Box Five."

"I wanted to talk to you about it, sir, so that you

mightn't have the same unpleasantness as Monsieur Debienne and Monsieur Poligny had. They wouldn't listen to me, at first."

"I'm not asking you about all that. I'm asking you what happened last night."

Madame Giry turned purple with indignation. Never had she been spoken to like that! She rose as though to go, gathering up the folds of her skirt and waving the feathers of her dingy bonnet with dignity, but changing her mind, she sat down and said, in a haughty voice:

"I'll tell you what happened. The ghost has been annoyed again. He had to tell the people that the Box was taken."

It appeared that Madame Giry thought it quite natural that a voice should be heard telling the latecomers that the box was taken when it appeared to be empty. She could only explain this by saying that the voice belonged to the ghost. Nobody could see the ghost in his box, but everybody could hear him. She had often heard him and they could believe her, for she always spoke the truth.

"Have you spoken to the ghost, my good lady?"

"As I'm speaking to you now, *my good sir!*"

"And when the ghost speaks to you, what does he say?"

"As I hand him his programme, he tells me to bring him a footstool."

Richard burst out laughing, as did Montcharmin and Rémy.

"A ghost asking for a footstool! Then this ghost of yours is a woman?"

"No, he has a man's voice, but sometimes he brings a lady with him. He tells me that he is the Opera Ghost and that I must not be afraid. Often he leaves me a few francs or some sweets on the little shelf where I put his programme, but since people have begun to annoy him, he leaves me nothing at all."

"Thank you, Madame Giry. You can go."

Madame Giry bowed herself out with the dignity which never deserted her.

Left alone, the managers told each other of the idea which they both had in mind, which was that they should look into that little matter of Box Five for themselves. Meanwhile, Madame Giry, who was obviously mad, must be replaced.

CHAPTER V

The Enchanted Violin

After the famous gala night Christine Daaé did not sing for a while and Carlotta returned to her famous performances. Christine appeared frightened by her success and had been heard to say sadly, "I don't know myself when I sing."

She showed herself nowhere, and the Vicomte de Chagny tried in vain to meet her. He wrote to her, asking leave to call upon her, but had given up all hope of receiving a reply, when, one morning, she sent him the following note:

Monsieur,

I have *not* forgotten the little boy who went into the sea to rescue my scarf. I feel that I must write to you today, when I am going to Perros to fulfil a sacred duty. Tomorrow is the anniversary of the death of my poor father, whom you knew and who was very fond of you. He is buried there with his violin, in the graveyard of the little church, at the bottom of the slope where we used to play as children, beside the road where, when we were a little bigger, we said goodbye for the last time.

The Vicomte de Chagny hurriedly consulted a railway guide, dressed as quickly as he could, wrote a few lines for his valet to take to his brother and jumped into a cab which brought him to the Gare Montparnasse in time to catch an express train for Brittany.

He alighted at a place called Lannion and hurried to catch the coach for Perros. He was the only passenger. He questioned the driver and learnt that, the previous day, a young lady who looked like a Parisian had gone to Perros and put up at the inn known as the Setting Sun.

The nearer he drew to her, the more fondly he remembered the story of the little Swedish singer. And this was the story:

There was once, in a little market town not far from Upsala in Sweden, a peasant who lived with his family, tilling the earth during the week and singing in the choir on Sundays. This peasant had a little daughter to whom he taught the musical alphabet before she learnt how to read. Christine Daaé's father was a great musician, perhaps without knowing it. His reputation was widespread, and he was always invited to set the couples dancing at weddings and other festivals. His wife died when Christine was nearly six and the father, who now cared only for his daughter and his music, sold his patch of ground and went to Upsala in search of fame and fortune. He found nothing but poverty.

He returned to the country, wandering from fair to fair, strumming his Scandinavian melodies on his beloved fiddle, while his child, who never left his side, listened to him in ecstasy or sang to his playing. One day a certain Professor Valerius heard them at Limby Fair, and took them to Gothenburg. He said that the father was the best violinist he had ever heard and that the daughter might become a great singer. Christine's education and musical instruction was paid for by the professor. She made rapid progress and charmed everybody with her prettiness, her grace of manner and her eagerness to please.

When Valerius and his wife went to live in France, they took Daaé and Christine with them. Mamma Valerius treated Christine as her daughter. As for Daaé, he began to pine away with home sickness. He never went out of doors in Paris, but lived in a sort of dream which he kept up with his violin. For hours at a time, he remained locked up in his bedroom, fiddling and singing very, very softly. Sometimes, Mamma Valerius would come and listen behind the door, wipe away a tear, and go downstairs again on tiptoe, sighing for her Scandinavian skies.

Daaé seemed not to recover his strength until the summer, when the whole family went to stay at Perros in a faraway corner of Brittany, where the sea was of the same colour as in his own country. Sometimes, when there were Breton pilgrimages, or village festivals or dances he would take his fiddle, as in the old days. His daughter was allowed to go with him for a week and they went around the countryside playing and singing. They accepted no money and the people could not understand the conduct of this rustic fiddler, who tramped the roads with that pretty child who sang like an angel from Heaven. The people followed them from village to village.

One day, a little boy, who was out with his governess, made her take a longer walk than she intended, for he could not tear himself from the little girl whose pure, sweet voice seemed to bind him to her. They came to the shore of a creek which led to a golden beach. Christine was on the beach when a high wind blew her scarf out to sea. Christine gave a cry and put out her arms, but the scarf was already far on the waves. Then she heard a voice say:

"It's all right; I'll go and fetch your scarf for you."

And she saw a little boy running fast, in spite of the outcries and indignant protests of a respectable lady in black. The little boy ran into the sea, dressed as he was, and brought back her scarf. Boy and scarf were both soaked through. The lady in black made a great fuss, but Christine laughed merrily and kissed the little boy, who was none other than the Vicomte Raoul de Chagny who was staying at Lannion with his aunt.

During the season, they saw each other and played together almost every day. Sometimes, in the evening, Christine's father would sit with them and tell them legends of the land of the North. There was one story called *Little Lotte*. It started like this:

"Little Lotte thought of everything and nothing. Her hair was gold as the sun's rays and her soul as clear and blue as her eyes. She wheedled her mother, was kind to her doll, took great care of her frock and her little red shoes and her fiddle, but most of all loved, when she went to sleep, to hear the Angel of Music . . ."

While the old man told this story, Raoul looked at Christine's blue eyes and golden hair; and Christine thought that Lotte was very lucky to hear the Angel of Music when she went to sleep. The Angel of Music played a part in all Papa Daaé's tales; and he said that every great musician, every great singer received a visit from the Angel at least once in his life.

"No one ever sees the Angel, but he is heard by those who are meant to hear him and then their music puts all other human sounds to shame."

Little Christine asked her father if he had heard the Angel of Music. But Papa Daaé shook his head sadly, and then his eyes lit up, as he said:

"You will hear him one day, my child! When I am in Heaven, I will send him to you!" He was beginning to cough at that time. Autumn came and parted Raoul and Christine.

Three years later, they met again at Perros. Professor Valerius was dead, but his widow remained in France with Papa Daaé and his daughter.

Being older now, Raoul and Christine were shy of each other, but they were always together and when Raoul went away, he pressed a kiss on Christine's trembling lips and said:

"Mademoiselle, I shall never forget you!"

Soon after this, Christine's father died and suddenly with him she seemed to have lost her voice, her soul and her genius. She continued her singing lessons to please old Mamma Valerius but seemed to have lost interest in everything.

The first time that Raoul saw Christine at the Opera, he was charmed by her beauty which brought back sweet images of the past, but he was surprised by her singing; it was as though she didn't seem to care, as if she had lost her touch. He went often to listen to her, he followed her in the wings, he tried to attract her attention, but she did not seem to see him. She appeared, for that matter, to see nobody. Raoul suffered, for she was very beautiful, while he was shy and dared not confess his love. Then came that wonderful gala performance. She had sung like an angel from heaven and it completed the conquest of his heart.

And then there was that man's voice behind the door – "You must love me!" – and no one in the room . . .

Why did she laugh when he reminded her of their time as children together, when he had rescued her scarf? Why did she not recognize him? And why had she now written to him?

At last Raoul reached Perros and walked into the smoky parlour of the Setting Sun where he saw Christine standing before him, smiling and showing no astonishment.

"So you have come," she said. "I felt that I should find you here when I came back from mass. Someone told me so at the church."

"Who?" asked Raoul, taking her little hand in his.

"Why, my poor dead father!"

There was a silence, and then Raoul asked:

"Did your father tell you that I love you, Christine, and that I cannot live without you?"

Christine blushed to the eyes and turned away her head. In a trembling voice she said:

"Me? You are dreaming, my friend!"

And she burst out laughing to cover her embarrassment.

"Don't laugh, Christine; I am quite serious."

And she replied gravely:

"I did not send for you to tell me such things as that."

"Why did you send for me if you did not think I loved you? You knew I would come."

"I thought you would remember our games here, as children, in which my father so often joined. I really don't know what I thought. Perhaps I was wrong to write to you . . ."

There was something in Christine's attitude that struck Raoul as not quite natural. She was not annoyed with him: the tenderness in her eyes told him that. But why was this tenderness so sad? That was what he wished to know and what was irritating him . . .

"When you saw me in your dressing room, was that the first time you noticed me, Christine?"

She was incapable of lying:

"No," she said, "I had often seen you in your brother's box. And also by the stage."

"I thought so!" said Raoul. "But then why, when you saw me in your room, at your feet, reminding you that I had rescued your scarf from the sea, why did you answer me as though you did not know me and also why did you laugh?"

Raoul spoke roughly and was immediately ashamed of himself. He had no right to speak to Christine like that, but now he had gone too far and he continued angrily and unhappily. "Well, I will answer for you. It was because there was someone in the room who was in your way, Christine, someone who would be jealous!"

"If anyone was in my way, my friend," Christine broke

in coldly, "if anyone was in my way that evening, it was yourself, because I told you to leave the room!"

"Yes, so that you could remain with someone else!"

"What are you saying?" cried Christine excitedly. "Who is 'someone else'?"

"The man to whom you said, 'I sing only for you! Tonight, I gave you my soul and I am dead!'"

Christine seized Raoul's arm and clutched it with a strength which one would not have suspected in so frail a creature.

"Then you were listening behind the door?"

"Yes, because I love you . . . And I heard everything . . ."

"What did you hear?" And the young girl, becoming strangely calm, released Raoul's arm.

"He said to you, 'Christine, you must love me!'"

Christine grew deathly pale and said in a low voice:

"Go on! Tell me all you heard."

At an utter loss to understand, Raoul answered:

"I heard him reply, when you said that you had given him your soul, 'Your soul is a beautiful thing, child, and I thank you. No emperor ever received so fair a gift. The angels wept tonight.'"

Christine carried her hand to her heart and two great tears trickled, like two pearls, down her ivory cheeks . . .

"Christine!"

"Raoul!"

The young man tried to take her in his arms, but she escaped and fled away.

Raoul walked about miserably all day. He guessed that Christine would be in her room and wondered how long she would stay there. Towards evening, he went to the little church and said a prayer for Papa Daaé. Then he climbed a slope and sat down on the edge of the moor overlooking the sea. The wind fell with the evening. By now it was dark and icy cold, but he did not feel it. Suddenly he gave a start; someone had come up behind him. It was Christine.

"Listen, Raoul," she said. "I have decided to tell you something serious. Do you remember the legend of the Angel of Music?"

"I do indeed," said Raoul. "I believe it was here that your father first told it to us."

"And it was here that he said, 'When I am in heaven, my child, I will send him to you.' Well, Raoul, my father is in heaven, and I have been visited by the Angel of Music."

"I have no doubt of it," said the young man gravely, thinking she referred to her triumph at the Opera.

"Yes," she replied solemnly. "I have heard him in my dressing room. That is where he comes to give me my daily lesson. You have heard him too."

"I? I heard the Angel of Music?"

"Yes, the other evening, it was he who was talking when you were listening behind the door. I was astonished this morning when you told me that you could hear him too . . ."

Raoul burst out laughing. The first rays of the moon came out and shrouded the two young people in their light. Christine turned angrily to Raoul. Her eyes, usually so gentle, flashed fire:

"What are you laughing at? You think you heard a man's voice, I suppose? Well, Monsieur, I am an honest girl and I don't lock myself in my dressing room with men's voices. If you had opened the door, you would have seen that there was no one there!"

"That's true! I did open the door when you were gone, and I found no one in the room . . ."

"So you see! . . . Well?"

Raoul summoned all his courage:

"Well, Christine, I think that somebody is making a game of you."

She gave a cry and ran away. He ran after her, but in a tone of fierce anger, she called out:

"Leave me! Leave me!"

42

And she disappeared.

Raoul returned to the inn, feeling very weary, very low-spirited and very sad. He was told that Christine had gone to her bedroom saying that she would not be down for dinner. Raoul dined alone in a very gloomy mood. Then he went to his room and tried to read, went to bed and tried to sleep. There was no sound in the next room.

The hours passed slowly. It was about half-past eleven when he distinctly heard someone moving, with a light, stealthy step, in the room next to his. Christine had not gone to bed! Quickly he pulled on a coat and waited. His heart thumped in his chest when he heard Christine's door turn slowly on its hinges. Softly opening his own door, he saw Christine's white form, in the moonlight, slip along the passage. She went down the stairs and he leant over the baluster above her. Suddenly he heard two voices in rapid conversation. He caught one sentence:

"Don't lose the key."

It was the landlady's voice. The door facing the sea was opened and locked again. Then all was still.

Raoul ran back to his room and threw open the window. Christine's white form stood on the deserted quay.

There was a tree outside his window and the first floor of the inn was at no great height, so Raoul was easily able to climb down and follow Christine as she left the quay and walked quickly up the road. The church clock struck a quarter to twelve and he thought that this must have made her hurry, for she began almost to run and continued at that pace till she came to the churchyard. The gate was open and the moon, shining on snow which had fallen, showed that there was no one else in the churchyard.

Raoul saw Christine kneel down by her father's grave, make the sign of the cross and begin to pray. At that moment, it struck midnight. At the last stroke, Christine lifted her eyes to the sky and stretched out her arms and from nowhere came the most perfect violin music. Raoul knew that music; he and Christine had heard it as children, but even Papa Daaé had not played like this. It was truly divine.

Christine walked slowly to the gate and Raoul was about to follow her when he saw a shadow suddenly glide along the sacristy wall. He ran up. The shadow had already pushed open the door and entered the church. But the young man was quicker and caught hold of a corner of its cloak. They were just in front of the high altar, and the moonbeams fell straight down through the stained glass windows of the apse. Raoul did not let go of the cloak, the shadow turned round, and he saw a terrible death's head, which darted a look at him from a pair of scorching yellow eyes. He felt as if he were face to face with the Devil. His courage failed him, he fainted and remembered nothing more until he recovered consciousness at the Setting Sun.

Great was the amazement of the landlady when, the next morning, the young man was brought back to her half frozen, more dead than alive, having been found stretched at full length on the steps of the high altar of the little church. She ran at once to tell Christine, who hurried down and, with the landlady, did her best to revive him. He soon opened his eyes and was not long in recovering when he saw his friend's charming face bent over him.

CHAPTER VI

The Fatal Performance

The two managers were about to carry out their decision to look into the matter of Box Five themselves and made their way, at a time when the house was empty, to the grand tier.

Box Five was just like all the grand tier boxes. There was nothing to distinguish it from any of the others. Monsieur Montcharmin and Monsieur Richard, making a show of being highly amused and laughing at each other, moved the furniture of the box, lifted the covers and the chairs and particularly examined the armchair in which the "voice" used to sit. But they saw that it was a respectable armchair, with no magic about it. Altogether, the box was the most ordinary box in the world, with its red hangings, its chairs, its carpets and its ledge covered in red velvet. After feeling the carpet in the most serious manner possible and discovering nothing there or anywhere else, they went down to the box immediately below on the pit tier. There they found nothing worth mentioning either.

"Those people are all making fools of us!" exclaimed Firmin Richard. "They are doing *Faust* on Saturday: let us both watch the performance from Box Five on the grand tier!"

On the Saturday morning, on reaching their office, the managers found a letter from O. G., worded as follows:

My dear Managers,
    Is it to be war between us?
    If you still care for peace, you must keep to the following conditions:

1. You must give me back my private box and I shall expect to have it from tonight onwards.
2. The part of Margarita shall be sung tonight by Christine Daaé. Never mind about Carlotta: she will be ill.
3. I insist on having the good and loyal services of my box-keeper, Madame Giry. You must give her back her work.
4. Let me know by a letter given to Madame Giry if you accept the terms of the lease concerning my monthly allowance. I will let you know later how you are to pay it to me.
    If you refuse, you will give Faust *tonight in a house with a curse upon it.*
    Take my advice and be warned in time.
                                                O. G.

"Look here, I'm sick of him, dead sick of him!" shouted Richard, bringing his fists down on his office table. Unfortunately for her, Madame Giry came in at that moment. She entered without ceremony, holding a letter in her hand, and said hurriedly:

46

"I beg your pardon. Excuse me, gentlemen, but I had a letter this morning from the Opera Ghost. He told me to collect a letter that you would have for him." Then she saw Firmin Richard's face, and a terrible sight it was. He seemed ready to burst and, fearing for her dignity, she made a quick turn and sought the door, just escaping the imprint of the sole of his boot on the back of her black taffeta skirt. Madame Giry was outraged and the corridor rang with her indignant yells, her violent protests and threats.

About the same time, Carlotta, who had a small house of her own in the Rue St Honoré, rang for her maid, who brought her letters to her in bed. There was an unsigned one among them, written in red ink, in a hesitating, clumsy hand which ran:

"If you appear tonight, you must be prepared for a great misfortune at the moment when you open your mouth to sing . . . a misfortune worse than death."

The letter took away Carlotta's appetite for breakfast. She pushed back her hot chocolate, sat up in bed and thought hard. It was not the first letter of this kind which she had received, but she had never had such a threatening one before.

Her first thought was to blame poor Christine. She had been jealous of her ever since the gala performance and had been unkind to her on several occasions.

When Carlotta had finished thinking over the threat contained in the strange letter, she got up.

"We shall see," she said, adding a few swearwords in her native Spanish, with a determined air.

The first thing she saw, when looking through the window, was a hearse. She was very superstitious, and the hearse and the letter convinced her that she was running the most serious risk that night. She collected all her supporters, told them there was a plot against her and asked them to be sure and attend her performance that night.

It was five o'clock when the post brought her a second anonymous letter in the same handwriting as the first. It was short, and said simply:

"You have a bad cold. If you are wise, you will see that it is madness to try to sing tonight."

Carlotta sneered, shrugged her handsome shoulders and sang two or three notes to reassure herself.

Her friends were faithful to their promise. They were all at the Opera that night, but, looking round, could see nothing unusual except that the managers were there in Box Five and thought that perhaps they had come in case there should be any trouble. In fact, Monsieur Richard and Monsieur Montcharmin were thinking of nothing but their ghost.

The famous tenor, Carolus Fonta, had hardly finished Faust's first appeal to the power of darkness, when Richard, who was sitting in the ghost's own chair, the front chair on the right, leant over to his partner and asked him jokingly:

"Well, has the ghost whispered a word in your ear yet?"

"Wait, don't be in such a hurry!" replied Montcharmin, giggling. "The performance has only begun, and you know that the ghost does not usually come until the middle of the first act."

The first act passed without incident, which did not surprise Carlotta's friends, because Margarita does not sing in this act. As for the managers, they looked at each other when the curtain fell.

"That's one act gone," said Montcharmin.

"Yes, the ghost is late," said Richard.

"It's not a bad audience," said Montcharmin, "for a house with a 'curse' on it."

Monsieur Richard smiled and pointed to a fat, rather vulgar woman, dressed in black, with a man in a broadcloth frock coat on either side of her.

"Who on earth are those?" asked Montcharmin.

"Those, my dear fellow, are my concierge, her husband and her brother."

"Did you give them their tickets?"

"I did . . . My concierge has never been to the Opera – this is the first time – and, as she is now going to come every night, I wanted her to have a good seat, before spending her time showing other people to theirs."

Montcharmin asked what he meant, and Richard answered that he had persuaded his caretaker, in whom he had the greatest confidence, to come and take Madame Giry's place for a time. Yes, he would like to see if, with a new woman instead of the old lunatic to look after it, Box Five would become perfectly normal.

Richard glanced across at a box on the grand tier containing two men.

"There is the Comte de Chagny."

"And who is that pale young man beside him?"

"That's his brother, the vicomte."

"He ought to be in his bed. He looks ill."

The second act finished without incident and the managers left the box during the interval. When they returned, the first thing they saw was a box of English sweets on the little shelf of the ledge. Who had put it there? They asked the box-keepers, but none of them knew. Then they went back to the shelf and, next to the box of sweets, they found an opera glass. They looked at each other. They did not feel like laughing. Everything that Madame Giry had told them returned to their memory . . . and besides . . . besides they seemed to feel a curious kind of draught around them. . . . They sat down in silence.

The scene was Margarita's garden. Christine was playing a boy's part.

"Gentle flowers in the dew,
    Be message from me . . ."

As she sang these first two lines, with her bunch of roses and lilac in her hand, Christine, raising her head, saw the Vicomte de Chagny in his box, and, from that moment, her voice seemed less sure, less crystal-clear than usual. Something seemed to deaden and dull her singing . . .

"What a queer girl she is!" said one of Carlotta's friends. "The other day she was perfect, and tonight she's simply bleating. She has no experience, no training."

Raoul was crying quietly behind his hands. He thought only of the letter which he received on his return to Paris, where Christine, fleeing from Perros like a thief in the night, had arrived before him:

My dear old little playfellow,
You must have the courage not to see me again, not to speak to me again. If you love me just a little, do this for me, for me who will never forget you, my dear Raoul. My life depends upon it. Your life depends upon it.
Your little Christine

To thunders of applause, Carlotta made her entrance. She flung herself into her part, certain of her voice and her success, fearing nothing. Her songs were clapped and cheered, and her duet with Faust seemed about to bring her a new success, when suddenly . . . a terrible thing happened.

Faust had knelt on one knee:

"Let me gaze on the form before me,
    While from yonder ether blue,
Look how the star of eve, bright and tender,
lingers o'er me.
    To love thy beauty too!"

And Carlotta, as Margarita sang back,

"Oh how strange!
        Like a spell does the evening bind me . . ."

50

At that moment, at that identical moment, the terrible thing happened . . . Carlotta croaked like a toad:

"Co-ack!"

No one could believe it, the great singer Carlotta of all people! Everyone felt that the thing was not natural, that there was witchcraft behind it. Poor, wretched, despairing, crushed Carlotta!

In Box Five, Montcharmin and Richard had turned very pale. They were filled with dread. They felt the influence of the ghost. They felt his breath. Montcharmin's hair stood on end. Richard wiped the perspiration from his forehead. Yes, the ghost was there. They were sure there were three people in the box. . . . They trembled. . . . They thought of running away. . . . They dared not. . . . They dared not make a movement or exchange a word which might have told the ghost that they knew he was there.

Carlotta tried again:

> "And a deep languid charm
> I feel without alarm – Co-ack!
> With its melody enwind me – Co-ack!
> And all my heart subdue – Co-ack!"

The house broke into a wild tumult. The two managers collapsed in their chairs and dared not even turn round. The ghost was chuckling behind their backs! And at last, they distinctly heard his voice in their right ears, saying: *"She is singing tonight to bring the chandelier down!"*

With one accord, they raised their eyes to the ceiling and uttered a terrible cry. The chandelier, the immense mass of the chandelier, was slipping down, coming towards them at the call of that fiendish voice. Released from its hook, it plunged from the ceiling and came smashing into the middle of the stalls, amid a thousand shouts of terror. A wild rush for the doors followed.

The chandelier had crashed down upon the wretched woman who was to be the new keeper of Box Five!

CHAPTER VII

Madame Valerius

That tragic evening was a bad one for all concerned. Carlotta fell ill. As for Christine Daaé, she disappeared after the performance.

Raoul, of course, was the first to be astonished at her absence. He wrote to her at Madame Valerius's flat and received no reply. His grief increased and he ended by being seriously alarmed at never seeing her name on the programme. *Faust* was played without her.

He went to the managers, but they were in a state of gloom, received him in a manner which was less than friendly, and said that Christine was taking a holiday and they did not know when she would be back.

Raoul remembered that Christine had asked him not to get in touch with her, but he was uneasy. He decided to go to Mamma Valerius's flat and find out what was going on. Was Christine a victim and, if so, of whom was she a victim? This was the very sensible question he put to himself as he hurried to her home.

He trembled as he rang at a little flat in the Rue Notre-Dame-des-Victoires. The door was opened by the maid whom he had seen coming out of Christine's dressing room one evening. He asked if he could speak to Madame Valerius and was told that she was ill in bed and was not receiving visitors.

"Take in my card, please," he said.

The maid soon returned and showed him into a scantily-furnished drawing room, in which portraits of Professor Valerius and old Papa Daaé faced each other on the walls.

"Madame begs Monsieur le Vicomte to excuse her," said the maid. "She can only see him in her bedroom; the poor lady has lost the use of her legs."

Five minutes later, Raoul was ushered into an ill-lit room, where he recognized the good, kind face of Madame Valerius in the semi-darkness of an alcove. Her hair was quite white now, but her eyes had grown no older: never indeed had their expression been so bright, so pure, so child-like.

"Monsieur de Chagny!" she cried, putting out both her hands to her visitor. "Ah, it's heaven that sends you here! We can talk of *her*."

"But Madame, where *is* Christine?" asked Raoul.

And the old lady replied calmly:

"She is with her good angel."

"What good angel?"

"Why, the Angel of Music."

The vicomte dropped into a chair. Really? Christine was with the Angel of Music? And there lay Madame Valerius in bed, smiling at him and putting her finger to her lips, to warn him to be silent! And she added:

"You must not tell anybody!"

"You can rely on me," said Raoul, utterly confused.

"I know! I know I can!" said the old lady with a happy laugh. "Give me your hands as you used to do when you were a little boy. I am very fond of you, Monsieur Raoul, you know. And so is Christine very fond of you."

"Yes, she is," sighed the young man. He found difficulty in collecting his thoughts which dwelt on the Angel of Music, of whom Christine had spoken so strangely and on the death's head which he had seen in a sort of nightmare on the high altar at Perros.

He asked in a low voice:

"What makes you think that Christine is fond of me, Madame?"

"She used to speak of you every day."

"And what did she tell you?"

"She told me you had asked her to marry you. But Monsieur, did you think that Christine was free?"

"Is Christine engaged to be married to someone else?" asked Raoul in a choking voice.

"Why, no! . . . You know as well as I do that Christine couldn't marry, even if she wanted to! . . ."

"No, I don't know. Why can't Christine marry?"

"Because the Angel of Music forbids her to."

"He forbids her! . . . The Angel of Music forbids her to marry!"

"Well, he forbids her . . . without forbidding her. It's like this: he tells her that, if she got married, she would never hear him again. He would go away for ever."

"And how long has Christine known him?"

"About three months . . . Yes, it's quite three months since he began to give her lessons."

Raoul threw up his arms in a gesture of despair.

"The Angel of Music gives her lessons! . . . And where, pray?"

"Now that she has gone away with him, I can't say; but up to a fortnight ago, it was in Christine's dressing room. It would be impossible in this little flat. The whole house would hear them. At eight o'clock in the morning at the Opera, there is no one about, you see," said the old lady, as if this arrangement was the most natural thing in the world.

"I see! I see!" cried the vicomte.

And he hurriedly took leave of Madame Valerius, who asked herself if the young man was not a little off his head.

Raoul staggered home and passed the night in total despair.

His valet found him in the morning sitting on his bed. He had not undressed and the servant feared, at the sight of his face, that some disaster had occurred. Raoul snatched his letters from the man's hands. He had recognized Christine's paper and handwriting. She said:

Dear,
   Go to the masked ball at the Opera on the night after tomorrow. At twelve o'clock, be in the little room behind the chimneypiece of the big crush-room. Stand near the door. Don't mention this to a living soul. Wear a white cloak and see that you are well masked. As you love me, do not let yourself be recognized.
                                        Christine

CHAPTER VIII

At the Masked Ball

The envelope was covered with mud and was unstamped. It bore the words "To be handed to Monsieur le Vicomte Raoul de Chagny," followed by his address in pencil. It must have been flung out of a window or perhaps a carriage, Raoul guessed. He read it with fevered eyes, had a bath and his breakfast and went out to buy himself a costume. He did not know what to make of it all, but he did as Christine had asked and bought a white cloak.

The hour of the appointment came at last. With his face in a mask trimmed with long, thick lace and a big, white cloak, Raoul thought himself most ridiculous. However, he consoled himself with the thought that he would certainly never be recognized!

This ball was a big affair which took place every year some time before Shrovetide. Numbers of singers and dancers, fashionable people and those who went often to the Opera performances were there and when Raoul arrived at five minutes to midnight, there was a crowd of people who were making a tremendous din. He did not stop to look at the fantastic costumes displayed all the way up the marble staircase – one of the finest settings in the world – spoke to none of the masked revellers, crossed the big crush-room and, escaping from a mad whirl of dancers in which he was caught for a moment, he at last entered the room which Christine had mentioned in her letter. He found it crammed with people and the fun was fast and furious, but he managed to get to the far door, leant against a doorpost and waited.

Raoul did not wait long. A figure in a black cloak passed and gave a quick squeeze to the tips of his fingers. The figure was masked, of course, but he guessed it was Christine and followed her in silence.

His guide turned round from time to time to see if he was following, and so they passed through the great crush-room.

Raoul could not help noticing, as they made their way through with some difficulty, a group crowding a person whose disguise, eccentric air and skeleton look were causing a sensation. It was a man dressed all in scarlet, with a huge hat and feathers on the top of a wonderful death's head. From his shoulders hung an immense red-velvet cloak, which trailed along the floor like a king's train, and on this cloak was embroidered in gold letters, which everyone read and repeated aloud:

"Touch me not! I am Red Death!"

Then one person, greatly daring, did try to touch him . . . but a skeleton hand shot out of a crimson sleeve and violently seized his wrist, and he, feeling the clutch of the knuckle-bones, the furious grasp of death, uttered a cry of pain and terror. When Red Death released him at last, he ran away like a madman, pursued by the jeers of the bystanders.

It was at this moment that Raoul passed in front of Red Death, who had just happened to turn in his direction. And he nearly cried out, "The death's head of Perros!" He had recognized him! . . . He wanted to dart forwards, forgetting Christine, but she caught him by the arm in an agitated manner and dragged him away from the crush-room and its mad crowd.

Christine kept on turning round and, it seemed that twice she saw something which startled her, for she hurried her pace and Raoul's as though they were being pursued.

They went up two floors. Here, the stairs and corridors were almost deserted. Christine opened the door of a private box and beckoned to Raoul to follow her.

Then she closed the door behind them and warned him, in a whisper, to remain at the back of the box, and on no account to show himself. Raoul took off his mask. Christine kept on hers. And, when Raoul was about to ask her to remove it, he was surprised to see her put her ear to the partition and listen eagerly for a sound outside. Then she opened the door a little, looked out into the corridor and, in a low voice, said:

"He must have gone up higher."

Suddenly she exclaimed:

"He is coming down again!"

She tried to close the door, but Raoul prevented her, for he had seen, on the top step of the staircase that led to the floor above, *a red foot*, followed by another . . . and slowly, majestically, the whole scarlet costume of Red Death met his eyes. And he once more saw the death's head of Perros.

"It's he!" he exclaimed. "This time, he shall not escape me! . . ."

But Christine had slammed the door at the moment when Raoul was on the point of rushing out. He tried to push her aside, but, with a tragic gesture, she flung out her two arms, fixing a barrier of white flesh against the door.

"In the name of our love, Raoul, you shall not pass! . . ."

"You want him to escape," cried Raoul in anger. "What is all this?"

"I came to tell you, dear, and to say farewell, but you will not understand."

"What will I not understand? Why do you keep going away? What does it mean? You are free; you go about Paris; you come to the ball . . . Why do you not go home? . . . What have you been doing this past fortnight? . . . What is this tale about the Angel of Music, which you have been telling Mamma Valerius? She lies waiting for you at home. What is keeping you? I beg of you, Christine, to explain."

Christine simply took off her mask and said:

"Dear, it is a tragedy!"

Raoul now saw her face and could not keep back an exclamation of surprise and terror. Her fresh complexion was gone and she was deathly pale. She had shadows under her eyes. It was a face of sorrow.

"My dearest! My dearest!" he moaned, holding out his arms. But she put her mask on again and slipped away, forbidding him, with hand upraised to follow her.

He watched her till she was out of sight. Then he also went down among the crowd, hardly knowing what he was doing, with throbbing head and an aching heart, and, as he crossed the dance floor, he asked if anyone had seen Red Death. Yes, everyone had seen Red Death, but Raoul could not find him and, at 2 o'clock in the morning, he turned down the passage, behind the scenes, that led to Christine Daaé's dressing room.

His footsteps took him to that room where he had first known suffering. He tapped at the door. There was no answer. The room was empty. A gas-jet was burning, turned down low. He saw some letter paper on a little desk and thought of writing to Christine, but heard steps in the passage. He only had time to hide in the inner room, which was separated from the dressing room by a curtain . . .

Christine entered, took off her mask with a weary movement and flung it on the table. She sighed and let her pretty head fall into her two hands. Was she thinking of him? . . . No, for he heard her murmur:

"Poor Erik!"

At first he thought that he must be mistaken. To begin with, if anyone was to be pitied, it was he, Raoul. It would have been quite natural if she had said, "Poor Raoul" after what had happened between them. But, shaking her head, she repeated:

"Poor Erik!"

What had this Erik to do with Christine's sighs and why was she pitying Erik when Raoul was so unhappy?

Christine sat down and began to write so calmly that Raoul who was still shaken was painfully impressed.

"What coolness!" he said to himself.

She wrote on, filling two, three, four sheets. Suddenly she raised her head and hid the sheets. . . . She seemed to be listening. . . . Raoul also listened. . . . A faint singing seemed to come from the walls . . . yes, it was as though the walls themselves were singing! The song became plainer . . . now he could hear the words . . . the voice was very beautiful, very soft, very appealing . . . but, for all its softness, it remained a man's voice. It came nearer and nearer . . . it came through the wall . . . it approached . . . and now the voice was *in the room*, in front of Christine. Christine rose and spoke to the voice, as though speaking to someone beside her:

"Here I am, Erik," she said. "I am ready. But you are late."

Raoul, peeping from behind the curtain, could see no one but Christine. Her face lit up and a smile of happiness appeared upon her bloodless lips, a smile like that of sick people when they receive the first hope of recovery.

The voice without a body went on singing, and Raoul could understand how Christine was able to sing so beautifully under the influence of the mysterious and invisible singer.

The voice was singing the Wedding-night Song from *Romeo and Juliet*. Raoul saw Christine stretch out her arms as she had done in the churchyard at Perros to the invisible violin. And nothing could describe the passion with which the voice sang:

"Fate links thee to me for ever and a day!"

The strains went through Raoul's heart. He drew back the curtain that hid him and walked to where Christine stood. She herself was moving to the back of the room, the whole wall of which was occupied by a great mirror that reflected her image, but not his, for he was just behind and entirely covered by her.

"Fate links thee to me for ever and a day!"

Christine walked towards her image in the glass and the image came towards her. The two Christines – the real one and the reflection – ended by touching, and Raoul put out his arms to clasp the two in one embrace. But, by a sort of dazzling miracle that sent him staggering, Raoul was suddenly flung back, while an icy blast swept across his face; he saw not two, but four, eight, twenty Christines spinning round him, laughing at him and fleeing so swiftly that he could not touch one of them. At last, everything stood still again, and he saw himself in the glass. But Christine had disappeared.

He rushed up to the glass. He struck at the walls. Nobody! And meanwhile the room still echoed with a distant passionate singing:

"Fate links thee to me for ever and a day!"

Worn-out, beaten, unable to think, Raoul sat down on the chair which Christine had just left. Like her, he let his head fall into his hands. When he raised it, the tears were streaming down his young cheeks, real, heavy tears like those which jealous children shed, a lover's tears, and he cried aloud:

"Who is this Erik?"

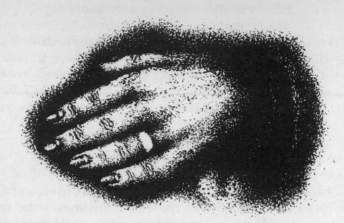

CHAPTER IX

The Gold Ring

The day after Christine had vanished before his eyes, Raoul called on Madame Valerius. He came upon a charming picture. Christine herself was seated by the bedside of the old lady, who was sitting up against her pillows, knitting. The pink and white had returned to the young girl's cheeks. The dark rings round her eyes had disappeared and Raoul no longer recognized the tragic face of the day before.

Christine rose and offered him her hand, but he was so amazed that he stood there without a word and did not take it.

"Well, Monsieur de Chagny," exclaimed Madame Valerius, "don't you know our Christine? Her Angel has sent her back to us."

"Mamma," broke in Christine, "you know there is no such thing as the Angel of Music!"

"But, child, he gave you lessons for six months!"

"Mamma, I promised to explain everything one of these days, but you promised in return not to talk about it and not to ask me questions."

"Yes, provided that you promised never to leave me again! But have you promised that, Christine?"

"Mamma, all this cannot interest Monsieur de Chagny."

"On the contrary, Mademoiselle," said Raoul, "I am delighted to find you with your adopted mother, but very surprised after what you told me yesterday and what I was able to guess. I am afraid for you, afraid that this secrecy may be fatal to you."

At these words Mamma Valerius tossed about in her bed.

"What does this mean?" she cried. "Is Christine in danger?"

"Yes, Madame," said Raoul, bravely, in spite of the signs which Christine made to him.

"What is this danger?" cried the old lady, gasping for breath. "You must tell me everything, Christine."

"She is being deceived. An imposter is taking advantage of her."

"Is the Angel of Music an imposter?"

"She told you herself that there was no Angel of Music. There is a terrible mystery around us, Madame, around you, around Christine, worse by far than any ghosts or genii."

Mamma Valerius turned a terrified face to Christine, who had already run to her adopted mother and was holding her in her arms.

"Don't believe him, Mamma, don't believe him," she repeated.

"Then tell me you will never leave me again," implored the old lady.

Christine was silent and Raoul continued, "You must promise, Christine. We will promise not to ask any more questions, if you promise to let us take care of you."

"The only person who could ask me that," said Christine, "would be my husband. Well, I have no husband and I never mean to marry."

She threw out her hands to emphasize her words and Raoul turned pale, not because of what she had said, but because he had caught sight of a plain gold ring on Christine's finger:

"You have no husband and yet you wear a wedding ring!"

He tried to seize her hand, but she swiftly drew it back.

"That's a present," she said, blushing.

"Is it from your Angel of Music? Is it from Erik?"

Christine turned white as a sheet and stammered:

"Who told you his name was Erik?"

"You yourself!"

"How do you mean?"

"The other night when you went to your dressing room, I heard you say 'Poor Erik.' It was the night of the masked ball."

"This is the second time you have listened behind the door!"

"I was not behind the door. I was in the inner room."

"Oh Raoul, unhappy man," cried Christine in terror. "Do you want to be killed?"

"Perhaps." He said this with so much love and despair in his voice that Christine could not keep back a sob. She took his hands and looked at him with deep affection.

"Forget the mystery. Do not try to solve it. Swear to me that you will never come to my dressing room again, unless I send for you."

"Then you promise to send for me sometimes, Christine?"

"I promise."

"When?"

"Tomorrow."

"Then I swear to do as you ask."

He bade farewell to the old lady, kissed Christine's hands and went away, cursing Erik but resolving to be patient.

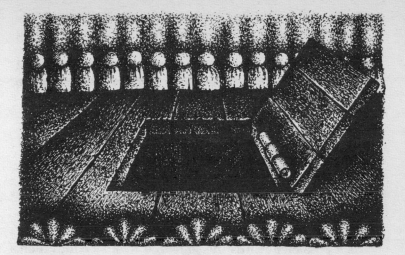

CHAPTER X

The Trap Door

The next day he saw her at the Opera. She was still wearing the plain gold ring. She was gentle and kind to him and they went for a walk. They went all around the Opera House which was an amazing place. They went up inside the roof where the scenery hung, all among the ropes and pulleys; they went to the little girls' dancing school, where children as young as six years old were practising their steps, in the hope of becoming great dancers one day. Meanwhile, Christine gave them sweets instead. They went to the wardrobe and property rooms and all over the immense building which was seventeen stories high.

Once, when they were passing before an open trap door on the stage, Raoul stopped and said:

"You have shown me all the upper part, Christine, except the roof, but there are strange stories told of the lower part . . . Shall we go down?"

She caught him in her arms, as though she feared to see him disappear down the black hole, and, in a trembling voice, whispered:

"Never! . . . I will not have you go there! Besides, it belongs to *him. Everything that is underground belongs to him.*"

Raoul looked her quickly in the eyes and said:

"So he lives down there, does he?"

"I never said so. Come along! Come!"

Christine was becoming agitated, so Raoul took her hand and she dragged him up to the topmost floor of the theatre, far, far from the trap door.

"I will remove you from his power, Christine, I swear it. And you shall not think of him any more."

"Is it possible?" Christine squeezed Raoul's hand, then, suddenly alarmed, turned away her head.

"Higher!" was all she said. "Higher still!"

She dragged him up towards the summit of the building. He had difficulty in following her. They slipped through the buttresses, the rafters, the joists; they ran from beam to beam as they might have run from tree to tree in a forest.

But, in spite of the care which she took to look behind her at every moment, she failed to see a shadow which followed her like her own shadow, which stopped when she stopped, which started again when she did and which made no more noise than a well-conducted shadow should. As for Raoul, he saw nothing either, for, when he had Christine in front of him, nothing behind him mattered.

CHAPTER XI

On the Roof

In this way they reached the roof. Christine tripped over it as lightly as a swallow. They could see over the whole of Paris. It was a gorgeous spring evening and they sat down side by side and he held her hand.

"I am going to take you away, Christine."

"I will come, dearest, but if, when the time comes, I refuse to go with you, well then, Raoul, you must carry me off by force!"

"Are you afraid that you will change your mind, Christine?"

"I don't know," she said, "he is a demon." And she shivered and nestled in his arms. "I am afraid now of going back to live with him . . . in the ground!"

"What makes you go back, Christine?"

"If I do not go, he will come and fetch me with his voice. And he will drag me with him, underground, and go on his knees before me, with his horrible death's head. And he will tell me that he loves me! And he will cry! Oh, those tears, Raoul, those tears in the two black eye-sockets of the death's head! I cannot see those tears flow again!"

"No, no, you shall never again hear him tell you that he loves you! You shall not see his tears! Let us fly, Christine, let us fly at once!"

"No," she said sadly, "it would be too cruel. Let him hear me sing tomorrow evening, and then we will go away. You must come and fetch me in my dressing room at midnight exactly. He will be waiting for me in the dining room by the lake: we shall be free and you shall take me away."

"How did all this start?" said Raoul. "Tell me how you saw him first."

"I heard him for three months without seeing him. The first time I heard it, I thought that that adorable voice was singing in another room. I went out, and looked everywhere, but, as you know, Raoul, my dressing room is a long way from the others, and I could not find the voice outside my room, whereas it went on steadily inside. It not only sang, but it spoke to me and answered my questions. The voice was as beautiful as the voice of an angel. I had never forgotten the Angel of Music whom my poor father promised to send to me as soon as he was dead. I really think that Mamma Valerius was a little bit to blame. I told her about it, and she at once said, 'It must be the Angel of Music. At any rate, you can do no harm by asking him.' I did so, and the man's voice replied that yes, it was the Angel's voice, the voice which I was expecting and which my father had promised me. From that time onward, the voice and I became great friends. It asked leave to give me singing lessons every day. I agreed, and, in a few weeks' time, I hardly knew myself when I sang and the voice said, 'Wait and see: we shall astonish Paris.'

"It was about then that I saw you for the first time, one evening, in the audience. I was so glad that I never thought of concealing my delight when I reached my dressing room. Unfortunately, the voice was there before me and soon noticed that something had happened to me. It asked me why I seemed so especially happy, and without thinking, I told it that I had given my heart to a young man I had seen in the audience. Then the voice was silent. I called to it, but it did not reply. I begged and entreated, but in vain. I was terrified it had gone for good. I wish to heaven it had! That night, I went home in a dreadful state. I told Mamma Valerius, who said, 'Why, of course, the voice is jealous!' And that, dear, first told me that I loved you . . ."

Christine stopped and laid her head on Raoul's shoulder. They sat like that for a moment, in silence, and they did not see the movement, at a few steps from them, of the creeping shadow of two great black wings, a shadow that came along the roof so near, that it could have closed over them and stifled them . . .

"The next day," Christine continued, "the voice told me I must choose between you and him. I still had faith in him and was terrified of losing him, especially as I believed my father had sent him. Also, I know your position in society as the Vicomte de Chagny, was not even sure if you remembered me from the old days and did not think there was any possibility of ever marrying you. So I told the voice you were no more than a brother to me and that my heart was not capable of earthly love. And that was why I refused to recognize or see you, when I met you on the stage or in the passages.

"Then, on that famous day, the voice said to me, 'Tonight, Christine, you can give to men a little of the music of Heaven!' . . . I don't know how it was that Carlotta did not come to the theatre that night nor why they called upon me to take her place, but I sang with a rapture I had never felt before and I felt for a moment as if my soul were leaving my body!"

"Oh, Christine," said Raoul, "I saw the tears stream down your cheeks and my heart wept with you. How could you sing like that while you were crying?"

"I felt myself fainting," said Christine. "I closed my eyes. . . . When I opened them, you were by my side. But *he* was there as well. I was afraid for your sake and again I pretended not to recognize you and began to laugh when you reminded me that you had rescued my scarf from the sea. Alas, there is no deceiving the voice! The voice recognized you and was jealous! It said that it was because I loved you that I avoided you; otherwise I would treat you like any other old friend. It went on and on, and at last I said, 'That will do! I am going to Perros tomorrow, to pray on my father's grave, and I shall ask Monsieur Raoul de Chagny to go with me.'

" 'Do as you please,' replied the voice, 'but I shall be at Perros too, for I am wherever you are, Christine, and if you are still worthy of me, if you have not lied to me, I will play for you at the stroke of midnight, on your father's tomb and on your father's violin.' That was how I came to write you the letter which brought you to Perros. Why did I not suspect? How was it, when I saw the selfish attitude of the voice, that I did not suspect him? Alas, I was no longer mistress of myself. I had become his thing."

"But after all," said Raoul, "you soon came to know the truth. Why did you not rid yourself of the nightmare?"

"Pity me, Raoul. It was like this:

"You remember the terrible evening when Carlotta thought she had been turned into a toad on the stage and when the house was plunged into darkness through the chandelier crashing to the floor and killing that poor woman? My first thought was for you and the voice. Well, I had seen you in your brother's box and I knew you were not in danger. But the voice had told me that it would be at the performance and I was really afraid for it, just as if it had been an ordinary person who might be dying. I thought to myself, 'The chandelier may have come down upon the voice.' I was then on the stage and was nearly running to look among the injured, when I thought that, if the voice was safe, it would be sure to be in my dressing room. I rushed to my room and there it was singing. It seemed to be calling me, I followed and – this is the extraordinary thing – my dressing room, as I moved, seemed to lengthen out. It must have been an effect done with mirrors, for I had the big mirror in front of me . . . And suddenly I was outside the room without knowing how! You, who saw me disappear from my room one evening, may be able to explain it, but I cannot."

"Where did the voice lead you?"

"Underground. I found myself in a boat on an underground lake. I knew that such a lake existed beneath the Opera, but I had never seen it. A man in a large cloak and in a mask was at the oars. He rowed with a quick, powerful stroke and his eyes, under the mask, never left me. We slipped across the noiseless water in a kind of bluey-light. Then we were in the dark again and we touched shore.

"I was taken up in the man's arms. I cried aloud. And then, suddenly, I was silent, dazed by the light . . . Yes, a dazzling light in the midst of which I had been set down.

"I sprang to my feet. I was in the middle of a drawing room that seemed to me to be decorated, adorned and furnished with nothing but flowers. They were cut flowers, wired and tied with silk ribbons, much too elegant, like those I used to find in my dressing room after a first night. In the midst of all these flowers, stood the black shape of the man in the mask, with arms crossed, and he said, 'Don't be afraid, Christine, you are in no danger.' It was the voice! . . . My rage equalled my amazement. I rushed at the mask and tried to snatch it away, so as to see the face of the voice. The man said, 'You are in no danger, so long as you do not touch the mask.' And, taking me gently by the wrists, he forced me into a chair and then went down on his knees and said no more.

"My courage started to come back and I began to look around the room. However extraordinary the adventure might be, I was in an ordinary room furnished with

71

perfectly ordinary things. I could almost have said where they came from and what they had cost. And the voice, the voice which I had recognized under the mask, was on its knees before me, *was a man*. I began to cry . . . The man, still kneeling, must have understood the cause of my tears, for he said, 'It is true, Christine! . . . I am not an angel, nor a ghost . . . I am Erik!' "

"Christine! Christine! Something tells me that we are wrong to wait. We should fly at once."

"If he does not hear me sing tomorrow, it will cause him great sorrow."

"But, in any case, it will cause him pain when you escape."

"You are right in that, Raoul, for certainly our flight will kill him. But then it counts both ways, for we risk his killing us."

"Does he love you so much?"

"He would commit murder for me."

"I hate him. Now that we know he is not a ghost, I would like to challenge him in his lair. Do you hate him, Christine?"

"No, but he fills me with horror. You see, I was angry with him for keeping me, and I tore off his mask. I am frightened, so frightened."

"You are frightened, but do you love me? If Erik were good-looking, would you love me, Christine?" He stood up and looked down at her.

She rose in her turn, put her two trembling arms round the young man's neck, and said:

"Oh, my dear, if I did not love you, I would not give you my lips!"

He kissed her lips, but the night that surrounded them was rent asunder. They fled as if a storm was coming and their eyes, filled with dread of Erik, showed them before they disappeared under the roof, high up above them, an immense night-bird, clinging to a pinnacle and staring at them with blazing yellow eyes.

CHAPTER XII

The Big Black Bird

Raoul and Christine ran and ran, eager to escape from the roof and the blazing eyes that showed only in the dark, and they did not stop before they came to the eighth floor on the way down.

There was no performance at the Opera that night and the passages were empty. Suddenly, a queer-looking form stood before them and blocked the way.

"No, not this way!"

And the form pointed to another passage by which they could reach the wings. Raoul wanted to stop and ask for an explanation. But the form, which wore a sort of long frock coat and a pointed cap, said:

"Quick! Go away quickly!"

Christine was already dragging Raoul along, so that he had to start running again.

"But who is he? Who is that man?" he asked.

Christine replied:

"It's the Persian."

"What's he doing here?"

"I don't know . . . He is always in the Opera . . ."

Presently, they came to Christine's dressing room.

"Why do you think you are safer in this room than on the stage?" asked Raoul. "You heard him through the walls; therefore he can hear us."

"No, he gave me his word not to be behind the walls of my dressing room again and I believe Erik's word. This room and my bedroom in the house by the lake are only for me, and not to be approached by him."

"How can you have gone from this room into that dark passage, Christine? Suppose we try to repeat your movements, shall we?"

"It is dangerous, dear, for the mirror might carry me off again; and instead of running away, I should be obliged to go to the end of the secret passage, to the lake and there call Erik."

"Would he hear you?"

"Erik will hear me wherever I call him."

"Well, I shall be here at twelve tomorrow night as we arranged. I shall keep my promise whatever happens. You say that, after listening to the performance, he is to wait for you in the dining room in the house by the lake?"

"Yes."

"And how does he think you are going to reach him, if you don't know how to go out by the mirror?"

"Why, by going straight to the edge of the lake."

Christine opened a box, took out an enormous key and showed it to Raoul.

"What's that for?" he asked.

"It is the key of the gate to the underground passage in the Rue Scribe. It leads straight to the lake."

Suddenly Christine went very pale.

"Oh heavens!" she cried, "the ring, the gold ring Erik gave me."

"Oh, so Erik gave you that ring!"

"You know he did, Raoul! But what you don't know is that, when he gave it to me, he said, 'I give you back your freedom, Christine, on condition that this ring is always on your finger. As long you keep it, you will be protected against all danger and Erik will remain your friend. But woe to you if ever you part with it, for Erik will have his revenge!' My dear, my dear, the ring is gone! . . . Woe upon us!"

They both looked for the ring, but could not find it. Christine refused to be comforted.

"It was while I gave you that kiss when we were up on the roof," she said. "It must have slipped from my finger and dropped into the street. We can never find it, and what misfortunes are in store for us now! Oh, to run away!"

"Let us run away at once," Raoul insisted, once more.

She hesitated. He thought she was going to say yes . . . Then her bright eyes dimmed and she said:

"No! Tomorrow!"

And she left him hurriedly.

Raoul went home, greatly concerned at all that he had heard.

"If I don't save her from the hands of that humbug," he said, aloud, as he went to bed, "she is lost. But I will save her."

He put out his lamp and felt a need to insult Erik in the dark, and he shouted:

"Humbug! . . . Humbug! . . . Humbug! . . ."

But suddenly, he raised himself on his elbow. Cold sweat poured down his face. Two eyes, like blazing coals, had appeared at the foot of his bed. They stared at him fixedly, terribly, in the darkness of the night.

Raoul was no coward, and yet he trembled. He put out a groping, hesitating, uncertain hand towards the table by his bedside. He found the matches and lit his candle. The eyes disappeared.

Still uneasy in his mind, he thought to himself:

"She told me that *his* eyes only showed in the dark. His eyes have disappeared in the light, but *he* may be there still."

And he rose, hunted about, went round the room. He looked under the bed like a child. Then he thought himself absurd, got into bed again and blew out the candle. The eyes reappeared.

Raoul sat up and stared back at them with all the courage he possessed. Then he cried:

"Is that you, Erik? Man or ghost, is it you?"

Then he thought to himself,

"If it's Erik, he's on the balcony!"

Then he ran to the chest of drawers and groped for his revolver. He opened the balcony window, looked out, saw nothing and closed the window again. He went back to bed, shivering, for the night was cold, and put the revolver on the table within his reach.

The eyes were still there, at the foot of the bed. Were they between the bed and the window-pane or behind the pane on the balcony? That was what Raoul wanted to know. Calmly he picked up his revolver and took aim. He aimed a little above the two eyes.

The shot made a terrible noise and wild footsteps came hurrying along the passages. Raoul sat up with out-stretched arm, ready to fire again if need be.

This time the two eyes had disappeared.

Servants appeared carrying lights; Count Philippe arrived, terribly anxious.

"What is it?"

"I think I have been dreaming," replied his brother. "I fired at two stars that kept me from sleeping."

"You're raving. Are you ill? For God's sake, tell me, Raoul, what happened?"

And the count seized hold of the revolver.

Raoul got out of bed and, opening the window, stepped out on the balcony. The count saw that the window had been pierced by a bullet at a man's height.

"My dear fellow," he said, "you have probably fired at a cat."

"That is quite possible," said Raoul, rubbing his hands. "With Erik you never know. Is it Erik? Is it the cat? Is it the ghost? With Erik, you can't tell."

He went on making these strange remarks and his brother wondered if he was going out of his mind.

"Who is Erik?" he asked, pressing Raoul's hand.

"He is my rival. And if he's not dead, it's a pity."

He dismissed the servants with a wave of his hand and the two brothers were left alone. But the men were not out of earshot before the count's valet heard Raoul say, distinctly and emphatically:

"I shall carry off Christine Daaé tonight."

During the night Raoul told his brother Christine's story and how he planned to save her. The brothers were devoted to each other, but Philippe did not approve of Raoul's plans and said so.

"You see, Raoul, you are making us ridiculous. That little girl has turned your head with her ghost stories." The only answer he received was:

"Goodbye, Philippe."

"Have you quite made up your mind? You are going tonight? With her?"

No reply.

"Surely you will not do anything so foolish? Mind you, I shall know how to stop you."

"Goodbye, Philippe," Raoul repeated and he left the room.

The brothers did not see each other again until that evening at the Opera. Raoul had spent the whole day making preparations for the flight. A travelling carriage had been hired and was waiting outside the theatre, with a coachman sitting on the box.

A shadow in a long black cloak and a soft black felt hat passed along the pavement, examined the coach carefully, went up to the horses and the coachman and moved away without saying a word.

They were performing *Faust* again and Christine, whose partner was Carolus Fonta, was not singing well. It was not until she saw Carlotta sitting with a sneering smile on her face in one of the boxes, that she made an effort, forgot her troubles and sang with all her heart and soul.

In the last act, when she began to sing to the angels, she made all the members of the audience feel as though they too had wings.

In the centre of the amphitheatre, a man stood up and remained standing, facing the singer. It was Raoul.

And Christine, her arms outstretched, her throat filled with music, the glory of her hair falling over her bare shoulders, uttered the divine cry:

"My spirit longs with thee to rest!"

It was at this moment that the stage was suddenly plunged into darkness. It happened so quickly that the spectators hardly had time to gasp, for the gas at once lit the stage again. . . . But Christine Daaé was no longer there! . . .

Raoul, still standing up in the amphitheatre, had given a cry. Count Philippe had sprung to his feet in his box. Raoul hurriedly went out, the count disappeared from his box, and the curtain was lowered. People flocked to the stage door to find out what had happened, while others stayed in their seats, all talking at once.

At last, the curtain rose slowly and Carolus Fonta stepped to the front of the stage and, in a sad and serious voice, said:

"Ladies and gentlemen, I have to tell you that our sister artiste, Christine Daaé, has disappeared before our eyes and nobody can tell us how!"

CHAPTER XIII

The Persian

Raoul was frantic with anxiety. He ransacked the Opera looking for Christine. He questioned everybody who might know what had happened to her, but nobody knew anything.

He ran outside. His own carriage was still there, but his brother's was missing! A bystander told him that the Comte de Chagny had flung himself into it and had shouted to his driver to make at all speed for the Brussels road.

Raoul thought immediately that his brother had arranged for Christine to be abducted to prevent him marrying her, and was going to some prearranged spot to collect her and take her out of the country.

He made straight for his travelling carriage, saying to himself, "I might just catch them."

A tall figure blocked his way:

"Where are you going so fast, Monsieur de Chagny?" asked a voice.

"Who are you?"

"You know who I am. I am the Persian. I am often here."

Raoul now remembered that his brother had once shown him that mysterious creature in the astrakhan cap, of whom nothing was known except that he was a Persian and that he lived in a little old-fashioned flat in the Rue de Rivoli.

The tall man bent over him:

"I repeat, Monsieur, where are you going so fast?"

"Can you not guess? To Christine Daaé's assistance, of course!"

"Then sir, stay here, for Christine Daaé is here!"

Raoul allowed himself to be led into a quiet corner of the building and said, "Here? With Erik?"

"With Erik."

"How do you know?"

"I was at the performance and no one in the world but Erik could do a trick like that! . . . Oh," he said, with a deep sigh, "I recognized the monster's touch! . . ."

"You know him then?"

The Persian heaved a fresh sigh. "I knew him in Persia."

"Sir," said Raoul, "can you do anything to help me? . . . I mean, to help Christine Daaé?"

"I think so, Monsieur de Chagny, and that is why I spoke to you."

"What can do you?"

"Try to take you to her . . . and to him."

"If you can do me that service, sir, my life is yours. I thought that Christine Daaé had been carried off by my brother, Count Philippe."

"Oh, Monsieur de Chagny, I don't believe a word of it."

"It's not possible, is it?"

"I don't know if it is possible or not, but there are ways and means of carrying people off, and Monsieur le Comte Philippe has never, as far as I know, had anything to do with witchcraft."

"Your arguments are convincing, sir, and I am a fool. I place myself in your hands. Let us be quick!"

"Then, sir," whispered the Persian, "let us not mention the name of Erik here. Let us say 'he' and 'him'; then there will be less danger of attracting his attention."

"Do you think he is near us?"

"It is quite possible, sir, if he is not, at this moment, with his victim, *in the house on the lake.*"

"Ah, so you know that house too?"

"If he is not there, he may be here, in the walls, in the floor, in the ceiling! . . . Come!"

And the Persian, asking Raoul to walk very quietly, led him down passages which Raoul had never seen before, even at the time when Christine had taken him all over the building.

"If only my servant Darius has come!" said the Persian.

After going up and down several staircases which were new to Raoul, the two men found themselves in front of a door which the Persian opened with a master-key.

"Your tall hat will be in your way, sir. You would do well to leave it in Christine Daaé's dressing room."

And the Persian, letting Raoul through the door which he had just opened, showed him the singer's room opposite.

"How well you know the Opera, sir."

"Not so well as *he* does," said the Persian, modestly, and he pushed the young man into Christine's dressing room.

Closing the door, the Persian went to a very thin partition that separated the dressing room from a big lumber room next to it. He listened and then coughed loudly.

There was a sound of someone stirring in the lumber room, and, a few seconds later, a finger tapped at the door.

"Come in," said the Persian.

A man entered, also wearing an astrakhan cap and

dressed in a long overcoat. He bowed, took a richly-carved case from under his coat, put it on the dressing table, bowed once again and went to the door.

"Did no one see you come in, Darius?"

"No, master."

"Let no one see you go out."

The servant glanced down the passage and swiftly disappeared.

The Persian opened the case. It contained a pair of long pistols.

· "When Christine Daaé was carried off, sir, I sent word to my servant to bring me these pistols. I have had them a long time and they can be relied upon."

"Do you mean to fight a duel?" asked Raoul.

"It will certainly be a duel which we shall have to fight," said the Persian, examining the priming of his pistols. "And what a duel!" Handing one of the pistols to Raoul, he added, "In this duel we shall be two to one, but you must be prepared for everything, for we shall be fighting the most terrible adversary that you can imagine. But you love Christine Daaé, do you not?"

"I worship the ground she walks on! But you, sir, who do not love her, tell me why I find you ready to risk your life for her! . . . You must certainly hate Erik!"

"No, sir," said the Persian sadly, "I do not hate him. If I hated him, he would long ago have ceased to do harm."

"Has he done you harm?"

"I have forgiven him the harm which he has done me."

"I do not understand you. You treat him as a monster, you speak of his crimes, he has done you harm and I find in you the same unexplained pity that drove me to despair when I saw it in Christine!"

The Persian did not reply. He fetched a stool and set it against the wall facing the great mirror that filled the whole of the partition opposite. Then he climbed on the stool and, with his nose to the wallpaper, seemed to be looking for something.

"Ah," he said, after a long search, "I have it!"

And, raising his finger above his head, he pressed against a corner in the pattern of the paper. Then he turned round and jumped off the stool.

"In half a minute," he said, "we shall be *on his path*!"

And, crossing the whole length of the dressing room, he felt the great mirror.

"No, it is not yielding yet," he muttered.

"Are you going out by the mirror?" asked Raoul. "Like Christine Daaé?"

"So you knew that Christine Daaé went out by the mirror?"

"She did so before my eyes, sir! . . . I was hidden behind the curtains of the inner room and I saw her vanish, not by the glass, but *in* the glass!"

"And what did you do?"

"I thought I was having some kind of a mad dream."

Bearing against the mirror, after a short silence, the Persian said:

"It takes some time to release the counter-balance, when you press on the spring from the inside of the room. It is different when you are behind the wall and can act directly on the counter-balance. Then the mirror turns at once and moves incredibly quickly on its pivot."

"It is not turning," said Raoul impatiently, "let us find another way."

"Tonight, there is no other way," said the Persian. "Look out! And be ready to fire!"

He himself raised his pistol opposite the glass. Raoul imitated his movement. With his free arm, the Persian drew the young man closer to him, and, suddenly, the mirror turned, in a blinding daze of cross-lights: it turned like a revolving door, carrying Raoul and the Persian with it and suddenly hurling them from the full light into the deepest darkness.

CHAPTER XIV

The Flaming Head

"Your hand high, ready to fire!" repeated Raoul's companion, quickly.

The wall behind them, having completed its circle, closed again, and the two men stood motionless for a moment, holding their breaths.

At last, the Persian decided to make a movement, and Raoul heard him slip on to his knees and feel for something in the dark with his groping hands. Suddenly, the dimness was made visible by a small dark lantern. The little red disc was turned in every direction and Raoul saw that the floor, the walls and the ceiling were all formed of planking. It must have been the usual way taken by Erik to reach Christine's dressing room.

The Persian went on his knees again and put his lantern on the ground. He seemed to be working at the floor.

Suddenly he turned off his light. Then Raoul heard a faint click and saw a very pale luminous square in the floor of the passage. It was as though a window had opened on the Opera cellars, which were still lit. Raoul no longer saw the Persian, but felt him by his side and heard his breathing.

"Follow me and do all that I do."

Raoul turned to the luminous aperture. Then he saw the Persian, who was still on his knees, hang by his hands from the rim of the opening, with his pistol between his teeth, and slide into the cellar below. Raoul followed and hung from the trap with both hands.

"Let go!" said a voice.

And he dropped into the arms of the Persian who reminded him to resume his firing position.

"My hand is getting tired," whispered Raoul, "if I have to fire, I shall not be sure of my aim."

"Then shift your pistol to the other hand," said the Persian.

"I can't shoot with my left hand."

"Then hold one of your hands as though you were going to pull the trigger of a pistol, with your arm bent, and put the pistol in your pocket. Silence now, and follow me."

The cellars of the Opera are enormous and they are five in number. Raoul followed the Persian and wondered what he would have done without his companion in that extraordinary labyrinth. They went down to the third cellar and, the lower they went, the more precautions the Persian seemed to take. He kept on turning to Raoul to see if he was holding his arm properly, showing how he himself carried his hand as if always ready to fire, though the pistol was in his pocket.

They were not alone for long. Shadowy figures came down from above. Each one carried a little lantern and moved it about, above, below and all around, as though looking for something or somebody.

"Bother!" muttered the Persian. "I don't know what they are looking for, but they might easily find us. Let us get away quickly." And he dragged Raoul down to the fourth cellar and from there down some steps to the fifth cellar.

Once in the fifth cellar, the Persian drew breath. He seemed to have a greater sense of security than he had displayed when they stopped in the third cellar, but he never failed to keep his hand up as if he was about to fire.

Then the Persian had a thought. Telling Raoul to stay where he was, he ran up a few steps of the staircase which they had just left and then returned.

"How stupid of us," he whispered. "We shall soon have seen the end of those men with their lanterns. It is the firemen going their rounds."

The two men waited five minutes longer. Then the Persian took Raoul up the stairs again, but then a fantastic face came in sight . . . a whole, fiery, frightening face.

Yes, a head of fire came towards them, at a man's height, but with no body attached to it. The face shed fire, looked in the darkness like a flame shaped as a man's face.

"Oh!" said the Persian between his teeth. "I have never seen *this* before. Pampin the fireman was not mad then, after all; he *did* see it! What can that flame be? It is not *he*, but he may have sent it! Come, let us run . . . it is safer." And they fled down the long passage that opened before them.

They continued to retreat, but the fiery face came on, gaining upon them. They could see its features clearly now. The eyes were round and staring, the nose a little crooked and the mouth large, with a hanging lower lip, very like the eyes, nose and lip of the moon, when the moon is quite red, bright red.

How did that red moon manage to glide through the darkness, at a man's height, with, apparently, nothing to support it? And how did it go so fast, so straight before it, with such staring, staring eyes? And what was that scratching, scraping, grating sound which it brought with it?

The Persian and Raoul could retreat no farther and flattened themselves against the wall, not knowing what was going to happen because there were hundreds of tiny sounds that moved in the darkness under the fiery face.

Then the two companions, flat against the wall, felt their hair stand on end with horror, for they now knew what the noises meant. They cried out, but the head of fire which was now level, turned round and spoke to them:

"Don't move! Don't move! Whatever you do, don't come after me! I am the rat-catcher. Let me pass, with my rats! . . ."

And the head of fire disappeared, vanished in the darkness, while the passage in front of it lit up, as the result of the change which the rat-catcher had made in his dark lantern. Before, so as not to scare the rats in front of him, he had turned his dark lantern on himself, lighting up his own head; now, to hasten their flight, he lit the dark space in front of him . . . And he sprang along, dragging with him his dreadful rats.

Raoul and the Persian breathed again, though still trembling.

"I ought to have remembered that Erik talked to me about the rat-catcher," said the Persian. "But he never told me that the man looked like that . . . and it's funny that I should never have met him before. . . . Of course Erik never comes to this part."

"Are we very far from the lake, sir?" asked Raoul. "Please, take me to the lake and then we can rescue Christine."

"Impossible!" said the Persian. "We shall never enter the house on the lake *by* the lake. I myself have never landed on the bank on which the house stands. One piece of advice, sir, never go near the lake . . . And, above all, shut your ears if you hear the voice singing under the water, the siren's voice!"

"But then what are we here for?" asked Raoul, overtaken by impatience and rage. "If you can do nothing for Christine, at least let me die for her!"

The Persian tried to calm the young man:

"We have only one means of saving Christine Daaé, believe me, which is to enter the house unperceived by the monster."

"And is there any hope of that, sir?"

"Ah, if I had not that hope, I would not have come to fetch you."

"And how can one enter the house on the lake without crossing the lake?"

"From the third cellar, from which we were so unluckily driven away. We will go back there now. I will show you the exact place; it is between two bits of scenery, exactly at the spot where Joseph Buquet died. Come sir, follow me."

The Persian darkened his lantern and led Raoul to the little staircase which they had been up before. They went up, stopping at each step, peering into the darkness and the silence, till they came to the third cellar. Here the Persian motioned to Raoul to go on his knees, and, in this way, crawling on two knees and one hand – for the other hand was still raised as if it had a pistol in it – they reached the end wall.

Against this wall stood two large pieces of scenery. Between them there was just room for a body . . . for a body which was found hanging there one day – the body of Joseph Buquet.

The Persian, still kneeling, stopped and listened. For a moment, he seemed to hesitate and looked at Raoul; then he turned his eyes up, towards the second cellar, which sent down the glimmer of a lantern through a cranny between two boards. This glimmer seemed to trouble the Persian.

At last, he tossed his head and made up his mind to act. He slipped between the two pieces of scenery, with Raoul close upon his heels. With his free hand, the Persian felt the wall. Raoul saw him bear heavily upon the wall, just as he had pressed against the wall in Christine's dressing room. Then a stone gave way, leaving a hole.

This time, the Persian took his pistol from his pocket and made a sign to Raoul to do as he did. He cocked the pistol.

And, resolutely, still on his knees, he wriggled through the hole in the wall. Raoul, who would have liked to pass through first, had to be content to follow him.

The hole was very narrow. The Persian stopped almost at once. Raoul heard him feeling the stone around him. Then the Persian took out his dark lantern again, stepped forward, examined something beneath him and immediately extinguished the lantern. Raoul heard him say, in a whisper:

"We shall have to drop a few yards, without making a noise. Take off your boots."

The Persian handed his own shoes to Raoul.

"Put them outside the wall," he said. "We shall find them there when we leave."

He crawled a little further on his knees, then turned right round and, facing Raoul, said:

"I am going to hang by my hands from the edge of the stone and let myself drop *into his house*. You must do exactly the same. Do not be afraid. I will catch you in my arms."

Raoul soon heard the dull sound of the Persian's fall and then dropped in his turn. The Persian caught him and they stood motionless, listening . . .

The darkness was thick around them, the silence heavy and terrible . . .

Then the Persian began to use the dark lantern again, turning the rays over their heads, looking for the hole through which they had come and failing to find it.

"Oh!" he said. "The stone has closed of itself!"

And the light of the lantern swept down the wall and over the floor.

The Persian stooped and picked up something, a sort of cord, which he examined for a second and flung away with horror.

"The Punjab lasso," he muttered. "It was against a throw from this that we had our arms up to protect our necks. This might very well be the rope by which the man Buquet was hanged. It disappeared after they took him down."

And, suddenly seized with a fresh anxiety, he moved the little red disc of his lantern over the walls. In this way, he lit up a curious thing: the trunk of a tree, which seemed still quite alive, with its leaves; and the branches of that tree ran right up the walls and disappeared in the ceiling.

Because of the smallness of that luminous disc, it was difficult at first to make out the appearance of things: they saw a corner of a branch . . . and a leaf . . . and another leaf . . . and, next to it, nothing at all, nothing but the ray of light that seemed to reflect itself . . . Raoul passed his hand over that reflection.

"Hullo!" he said. "This wall is a looking glass!"

"Yes, a looking glass," said the Persian, in a tone of deep feeling. And, passing the hand that held the pistol over his moist forehead, he added, "We have dropped into the torture chamber."

CHAPTER XV

Christine, a Captive

They were in the middle of a small six-cornered room, the sides of which were covered with mirrors from floor to ceiling. Raoul saw that the tree in the corner was not real, but made of iron. An iron branch stuck out from it, and he realized with horror that it was a gallows tree on which poor Joseph Buquet had almost certainly met his end, his body being found later among the scenery above.

Suddenly they heard voices on their left. It sounded at first like a door opening and shutting in the next room, and then came a dull moan. They heard voices:

"Christine, you must make your choice! Will you have a wedding mass or a requiem mass?"

They recognized the voice of the monster.

There was another moan, followed by a long silence.

The Persian restrained Raoul who wanted to rush through the walls to Christine Daaé, whose moans, as they thought, they continued to hear at intervals.

"The requiem mass is not at all festive," Erik's voice resumed, "whereas the wedding mass is magnificent! One must take a resolution and know one's mind. I can't go on living like this, like a mole in a burrow. I want to live like everybody else. I want to have a wife like everybody else and to take her out on Sundays. I have invented a mask that makes me look normal. People will not even turn round to stare at me. You will be the happiest of women. And we will sing, all by ourselves, till we swoon away with delight. You are crying! You are afraid of me! And yet I am not really wicked. Love me and you shall see! All I want is to be loved for myself. If you loved me, I should be as gentle as a lamb, and you could do anything with me that you pleased."

Soon the moans that accompanied this sort of love's litany increased and increased and they realized that this terrible lamentation came from Erik himself. They pictured Christine, standing dumb with horror, without strength to cry out, while the monster was on his knees before her.

There was a long silence and they said hopefully to themselves: "Perhaps he has left Christine, behind the wall."

They could not think how to tell Christine they were there, without Erik finding out. They were unable to leave the torture chamber, unless Christine opened the door to them, and they did not even know where the door might be.

Suddenly the silence in the next room was disturbed by the ringing of an electric bell. There was a bound on the other side of the wall and Erik's voice of thunder:

"Somebody ringing! Come in!"

A sinister chuckle:

"Who has come bothering me now? Wait for me here, Christine. I am going to open the door."

Steps moved away, a door closed. They had no time to think of the fresh horror that might be coming and that the monster might only be going out, perhaps, to commit a fresh crime. They thought of only one thing: that Christine was alone behind the wall!

Raoul was already calling to her:

"Christine! Christine!" he went on calling until a faint voice reached them:

"I am dreaming!" it said.

"Christine, Christine, it is I, Raoul!"

A silence.

"But answer me, Christine! In heaven's name, if you are alone, answer me!"

Then Christine's voice whispered Raoul's name.

"Yes, it is I! It is not a dream! We are here to save you, but be careful. When you hear Erik, warn us. The Persian is with me."

Then Christine told them that Erik had gone quite mad with love and that he had decided *to kill everybody and himself with everybody* if she did not consent to become his wife. He had given her until eleven o'clock the next evening to think about it. This was her last chance. She must then choose, as he said, between a wedding or a funeral.

And then Erik had uttered a phrase which Christine did not quite understand:

"Yes or no! If your answer is no, everybody will be dead *and buried."*

"Can you tell us where Erik is?" asked the Persian.

Christine replied that she thought he had left the house.

"Could you make sure?"

"No. I am fastened . . . I cannot move."

Raoul and the Persian looked at each other aghast. The safety of all three of them depended on Christine being free to move.

"Where are you?" asked Christine. "There are only two doors in my room: a door through which Erik comes and goes and another which he has never opened in front of me and which he has forbidden me ever to go through, because he says it is the most dangerous of the doors, the door of the torture chamber."

"Christine, that is where we are!"

"You are in the torture chamber?"

"Yes, but we cannot see the door."

"If I could only move, I would knock at the door and that would tell you where it is."

"Is it a door with a lock to it?" asked the Persian.

"Yes, with a lock."

"Mademoiselle," said the Persian, "it is absolutely necessary that you open that door to us."

"I know where the key is," whispered Christine, "but I cannot get to it." And she gave a sob.

"Mademoiselle, where is the key?"

"In the next room by the organ, with another little bronze key which he also forbade me to touch. They are both in a little leather bag which he calls the bag of life and death. But you must fly, both of you. Everything is mysterious and terrible here. Erik will soon have gone quite mad . . . and you are in the torture chamber. Go back by the way you came! There must be a reason why the room has that name!"

"Christine," said Raoul, "we will all three go from here together or die together."

"Mademoiselle," said the Persian, "the monster bound you and he shall unbind you. Remember that he loves you. Smile on him, entreat him, tell him that your bonds hurt you."

But Christine Daaé said:

"Hush! I hear something in the wall of the lake. It is Erik! Go away!"

Heavy steps dragged slowly behind the wall, stopped and then made the floor creak once more. Next came a tremendous sigh, followed by a cry of horror from Christine, and we heard Erik's voice:

"I beg your pardon for letting you see a face like this! What a state I am in, am I not? It's *the other man's* fault!

Why did he ring? Do *I* ask people who pass to tell me the time? Well, he will never ask anyone the time again!"

There was another deep sigh.

"Why did you cry out, Christine?"

"Because I am in pain, Erik."

"I thought I had frightened you."

"Erik, unloose my bonds. Am I not your prisoner?"

"Very well. In a minute I will release you. Are you looking at me because I am all wet? Oh, my dear, it's raining heavily outside. Apart from that, Christine, I believe I am suffering from hallucinations. You know the man – I wonder if he is ringing at the bottom of the lake – well, he was rather like someone we both know. There, turn round. You're free now. Oh, Christine, look at your poor dear wrists. Tell me, have I hurt them? That alone deserves death. Talking of death, I must sing his requiem!"

Raoul and the Persian looked at each other in horror. What poor wretch had strayed to the shore of the lake? Who was *the other man* whose requiem they now heard sung?

Erik sang like the god of thunder; the elements seemed to rage around them. Suddenly the organ and the voice ceased so suddenly that the two prisoners, on the other side of the wall, jumped back with the shock. And the voice now changed and transformed, distinctly grated out these metallic syllables:

"What have you done with my bag?"

CHAPTER XVI

In the Torture Chamber

The voice repeated angrily:

"What have you done with my bag? So it was to take my bag that you asked me to release you!"

They heard hurried steps, Christine running back to the Louis-Philippe room, as though to seek shelter in front of the torture chamber wall.

"What are you running away for?" asked the furious voice, which had followed her. "Give me back my bag, will you? Don't you know that it is the bag of life and death?"

"Listen to me, Erik," sighed the girl, "as it is settled that we are to live together, what difference can it make to you?"

"You know there are only two keys in it," said the monster. "What do you want to do?"

"I want to look at this room which I have never seen and which you have always kept hidden from me . . . It's woman's curiosity!" she said, in a tone which she tried to render playful.

But the trick was too childish for Erik to be taken in by it.

"I don't like curious women," he retorted, "and you had better remember the story of Bluebeard and be careful. Come, give me back my bag! Leave the key alone, will you, you inquisitive little thing!"

Erik chuckled while Christine gave a cry of pain . . . He had evidently recovered the bag from her.

At that moment, Raoul could not help uttering a cry of helpless rage.

"Hullo, what's that?" said the monster. "Did you hear something, Christine?"

"No, no!" replied the poor girl. "I heard nothing!"

"I thought I heard a cry."

"A cry! . . . Are you going mad, Erik? Whom do you expect to give a cry, in this house? I cried out, because you hurt me. I heard nothing."

"I don't like the way you said that . . . You're trembling. You're lying. There *was* a cry. There is someone in the torture chamber."

"No one, Erik."

"Someone. The man you want to marry, perhaps!"

"I don't want to marry anybody. You know I don't."

Another nasty chuckle:

"Well, it won't take long to find out. Christine, my love, we need not open the door of the torture chamber to see if there is anyone there. If there is someone, you will see the invisible window light up at the top of the wall, near the ceiling. We have only to draw back the black curtain and put out the light here. There, watch, I am putting out the light."

Raoul and his companion were suddenly flooded with light. On their side of the wall, everything seemed aglow. Raoul staggered where he stood, but the Persian, knowing the ways of Erik, seemed less surprised. Erik must have heard Raoul, for his angry voice roared out:

"I told you there was someone there. Do you see the

window, the lighted window, up there? The man behind the wall can't see it, but you shall go up the folding steps: that is what they are there for. You have often asked me to tell you, and now you know. They are there to give a peep into the torture chamber, you inquisitive little thing!"

"Erik, you are only trying to frighten me. There is no torture, is there?"

"Go and look through the little window, dear."

They heard the steps being dragged against the wall.

"Up with you. No? Then I will go up myself, dear."

"Oh, very well, I will go up."

"Oh, my darling, my darling! How sweet of you! How nice of you to save me the effort, at my age! Tell me what he looks like."

At that moment, Raoul and the Persian heard these words above their heads:

"There is no one there, Erik."

"No one? Are you sure?"

"I can see no one, but I can see a tree with a branch sticking out."

"Ah!" said the terrible voice, "that is my gibbet on which I hang people. That is why the room is called the torture chamber."

"Put out the light in the little window. Oh, Erik, do put out the light."

Christine's voice sounded faint and shocked, but the two men knew that, at least, she must have seen them and seen too that they were alive and well.

Christine seemed to have come down from the steps and Erik was now trying to take her mind off the torture chamber by playing ventriloquist's tricks. He could throw his voice anywhere and he demonstrated to Christine how he had made poor Carlotta croak like a toad, and how he had talked to Madame Giry from a hiding place in a hollow pillar near Box Five. He really was a very good ventriloquist. For a moment, Raoul even thought he was with them in the torture chamber. Then they heard Christine's voice:

"Erik, Erik, you tire me with your voice. Don't go on, Erik! . . . Isn't it very hot here?"

"Oh yes," replied Erik's voice, "the heat is unendurable."

"The wall is quite hot. Erik, the wall is burning!"

"Ah yes, Christine dear, and so is the torture chamber!"

CHAPTER XVII

Barrels! Barrels!

The walls of the torture chamber were lined with mirrors which soon began to give off immense heat until the perspiration began to pour down the faces of the two prisoners. Both knew they were in terrible danger and thought of nothing but the heat and how to escape.

To begin with, they abandoned all hope of getting back the way they had come in. They had dropped from too great a height into the torture chamber, and there was no furniture to help them reach the passage above; not even the branch of the iron tree, nor each other's shoulders would be any use.

There was only one possible outlet, that opening into the Louis-Philippe room where Erik and Christine had been. The Persian thought he had heard Erik dragging Christine away lest she should interfere with his wicked plans. No voices were heard. The door between the rooms was invisible to anyone in the torture chamber, so they therefore had to try and open it without even knowing where it was!

The heat was infernal and soon they were crawling on the floor, panting for water. As they rolled over in their agony, the Persian saw, in a groove in the floor, a black-headed nail whose use he thought he knew. He pressed the spring and called, in a whisper, to Raoul. The black-headed nail yielded to his pressure . . .

And then . . .

And then they saw, not the door opening in the wall, but a cellar-flap released in the floor. Cool air came up to them from the black hole below.

The Persian thrust his arm into the darkness and came upon a stone and another stone . . . a staircase . . . a dark staircase leading into the cellar. Raoul wanted to dash straight down the hole, but the Persian, fearing a new trick of the monster's, stopped him, turning on his dark lantern and went down first.

The staircase was a winding one and led down into pitch darkness. It was deliciously cool, and they felt the lake could not be far away.

They soon reached the bottom. Their eyes were beginning to accustom themselves to the dark, to distinguish shapes around them . . . circular shapes, on which the Persian turned the light of his lantern.

Barrels! . . .

They were in Erik's cellar. It was here that he must keep his wine and perhaps his drinking water.

There were quite a number of barrels, neatly arranged in two rows, one on either side of them. They were small barrels and the two explorers thought that Erik must have chosen them because they would be easy to transport to the house on the lake. They examined them all, hoping to find one that had already been tapped, so that they could have a drink, but they were all firmly sealed.

Then, after half lifting one to make sure that it was full, they went on their knees and, with a small knife which he carried, the Persian prepared to drive in the bung-hole. Raoul put his two hands together underneath it, and, with a great effort, the Persian burst the bung.

"What's this?" cried Raoul. "This isn't water, nor is it wine!" He put his two full hands close to the lantern . . . the Persian bent over to look and immediately flung away his lantern with such violence that it broke and went out, leaving them in utter darkness. What he had seen in Raoul's hands was gunpowder!

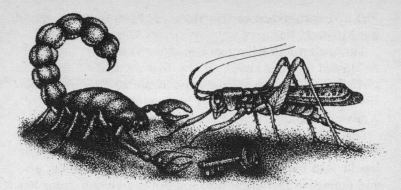

CHAPTER XVIII

The Scorpion and the Grasshopper

The discovery flung them into a state of alarm that made them forget all their past and present sufferings. They now knew what Erik meant when he said to Christine Daaé:

"Yes or no! If your answer is no, everybody will be dead *and buried.*"

Yes, buried under the ruins of the Paris Opera House!

The monster had given her until eleven o'clock in the evening. He had chosen his time well. There would be many people in the brilliant theatre. He would go to his death among the rich and famous. Raoul and his Persian friend and Erik would all be blown up during the middle of the performance if Christine Daaé said no!

Raoul and the Persian retraced their steps as quickly as they could manage in the dark, to get away from the barrels of gunpowder, although it meant going back to the horrible room of mirrors.

They found the staircase and rushed up it, stumbling as they went. The trap door was still open, but it was now as dark in the room of mirrors as in the cellar which they had just left.

They crawled across the floor of the torture chamber and listened.

Suddenly the Persian exclaimed:

"Hush!"

He thought he heard footsteps in the next room. Someone tapped against the wall. Christine's voice said:

"Raoul! Raoul!"

They now all began to talk at once, on either side of the wall. Christine sobbed: she had not felt sure that she would find Raoul alive. . . . Erik had been terrible, she told them. He had done nothing but rave, waiting for her promise to marry him, which she would not give. It went on for hours and hours until at last he had just gone out, leaving her to think about it for the last time.

"Hours and hours? What is the time now, Christine? We have lost all sense of time."

"It is eleven o'clock, all but five minutes."

"But which eleven o'clock?"

"The eleven o'clock which is to decide life or death. He told me so before he left. He is terrible; he is quite mad. He tore off his mask and his yellow eyes shot flames!

"Then he took a key out of his little bag of life and death and told me that it would open two ebony caskets in the Louis-Philippe room where I am now. The caskets are on the mantelpiece; one contains a scorpion, the other a grasshopper. If I turn the scorpion, it means yes, but the grasshopper means no. Then he laughed like a drunken demon and left me. His last words were: "Mind the grasshopper! It not only turns: it hops! . . . And it hops jolly high!"

The Persian, who understood Erik's inventive mind, had no doubt that the grasshopper controlled an electric current intended to blow up the gunpowder. At the same time, it was perfectly possible that he was deceiving Christine and that it was the scorpion which would blow everything up. He called out:

"Christine, where are you?"

"By the scorpion."

"Don't touch it!"

"Erik is back," cried Christine. "I hear him. Here he is!"

They heard his steps approaching the Louis-Philippe room. He came up to Christine, but did not speak.

The Persian raised his voice:

"Erik, it is I. Do you recognize my voice?"

With extraordinary calmness, he replied:

"So you are not dead in there? Well then, keep quiet!"

Raoul tried to speak, but Erik said coldly:

"Not a word either of you or I shall blow everything up."

There was silence and then he spoke again:

"Now Christine, I am opening the little ebony caskets. Look at the little dears inside. Aren't they pretty? . . . If you turn the grasshopper, my dear, we shall all be blown up. If you turn the scorpion, all that gunpowder will be soaked and drowned. All the people in the Opera House will be saved, and merrily, merrily we shall be married!"

There was a long pause. Raoul was on his knees praying and the Persian clutched his heart with both hands.

"If, in two minutes, Christine, you have not turned the scorpion, I shall turn the grasshopper, and the grasshopper, I tell you, *hops jolly high!*"

Another long silence. Then:

"The two minutes are past. You won't have the scorpion? Then I turn the grasshopper!"

"Erik!"

"Well?"

"I have turned the scorpion!"

They felt something crack beneath their feet and heard a hissing sound, like the first hiss of a rocket. It came softly at first, then louder, then very loud. It was not the hiss of fire: it was the hiss of water.

And now it became a gurgling sound.

They rushed to the trap door. All their thirst which had

vanished when the terror came, now returned with the lapping of the water.

The water rose in the cellar, above the barrels of gunpowder and they went down to it with parched throats. It rose to their chins, to their mouths. And they drank. They stood on the floor of the cellar and they drank. And they went up the stairs again in the dark, step by step, went up with the water.

The water came out of the cellar with them and spread over the floor of the room. If this went on, the whole house on the lake would be swamped. The floor of the torture chamber had itself become a regular little lake, in which their feet splashed. They called out:

"Erik! Erik! Turn off the tap! Turn off the scorpion!"

There was no reply. The water rose to their knees, to their shoulders. They began to whirl around in the water like so much wreckage. They tried to grasp the glass walls, but they slipped from under their groping fingers. They began to sink! One last effort! One last cry!

"Erik! Christine!"

They lost consciousness and only the gurgle of the water could be heard.

CHAPTER XIX

Poor Erik!

When the Persian opened his eyes, he found himself lying on a bed. Raoul was asleep on a sofa, beside the wardrobe and they were in Erik's room in the house by the lake at the bottom of the Opera cellars. To the Persian, it seemed like a dream, and the figure of the masked man seemed all the more formidable in this old-fashioned neat room with its ordinary, everyday furniture. Erik bent down and asked the Persian if he was better.

Meanwhile Christine Daaé did not say a word: she moved about noiselessly, like a sister of charity who had taken a vow of silence. She brought a cup of hot tea and the man in the mask took it from her hands and gave it to the Persian. Raoul was still sleeping. Erik left the room for a moment and the Persian raised himself on his elbow, looked around him and saw Christine Daaé sitting by the fireside. He spoke to her, but he was still very weak and he fell back on the pillow. Christine came to him, laid her hand on his forehead and went away again.

Erik returned with some little bottles which he placed on the mantelpiece. And, in a whisper, so as not to wake Raoul, he said to the Persian, after sitting down and feeling his pulse:

"You are now saved, both of you. And soon I shall take you up to the surface of the earth, *to please my wife.*"

Thereupon he rose, without further explanation, and disappeared once more.

Erik returned, gave the Persian a drink from one of the little bottles and advised him not to speak to *his wife* again or to anyone, *because it might be dangerous to everybody's health.*

Eventually, the Persian fell asleep like Raoul, and did not wake until he was in his own room, nursed by his faithful servant Darius, who told him that, on the night before, he was found propped against the door of his flat, where he had been brought by a stranger who rang the bell before going away.

As soon as the Persian recovered his strength, he sent Darius to Count Philippe's house to enquire after his brother's health. The answer came back that Raoul had not been seen and that Count Philippe was dead. His body was found on the bank of the Opera lake on the Rue-Scribe side. The Persian remembered the requiem which he had heard Erik singing, and he had no doubt regarding the crime and the criminal. Knowing Erik as he did, he easily reconstructed the tragedy:

Thinking that his brother had run away with Christine, Philippe must have dashed in pursuit of him down the Brussels road. Failing to find the pair, he hurried back to the Opera, remembered what Raoul had told him about his fantastic rival and learnt that his brother had made every effort to enter the cellars of the theatre and that he had disappeared, leaving his hat in Christine's dressing room beside an empty pistol-case. Count Philippe, who really thought Raoul must be out of his mind, followed him into that infernal underground maze. This was enough, the Persian thought, to explain the discovery of the Comte de Chagny's corpse by the side of the lake.

He was writing down what he knew for the police and had just finished when Darius announced the visit of a stranger who refused to give his name, who would not show his face and who declared simply that he did not intend to leave the place until he had spoken to his master.

The Persian guessed at once who the visitor was and ordered him to be shown in. He was right. It was the ghost; it was Erik.

He looked extremely weak and leant against the wall as though afraid of falling. Taking off his hat, he revealed a forehead white as wax. The rest of the face was hidden by the mask.

The Persian rose to his feet as Erik entered.

"Murderer of Count Philippe, what have you done with his brother and Christine Daaé?"

Erik staggered under the direct attack, kept silent for a moment, dragged himself to a chair and, gasping for breath, said:

"My friend, don't talk to me about Count Philippe. It was an accident. He fell into the lake."

"You lie!" shouted the Persian.

Erik bowed his head and said:

"I have not come here to talk about Count Philippe, but to tell you that I am going to die."

"Where are Raoul de Chagny and Christine Daaé?"

"I am going to die . . ."

"Raoul de Chagny and Christine Daaé?"

"Of love . . . I am dying of love. I loved her so and I love her still and I am dying of love for her. If you knew how beautiful she was when I kissed her, just on the forehead, and she did not draw back. She entreated me to save you both and said she would be my wife. She would not kill herself, as she had sometimes threatened. It was a bargain. Half a minute later, all the water was back in the lake, and I had a hard job with you, for, upon my honour, I thought you were done for! It was agreed that I should take you both up to the surface of the earth. When at last I cleared the Louis-Philippe room of you, I came back alone."

"What have you done with Raoul?" demanded the Persian.

"Ah, you see, I couldn't carry *him* up like that at once because *he* was a hostage. But I could not keep him in the house on the lake either, because of Christine, so I locked him up comfortably. I chained him up nicely in an old dungeon, which is in the most remote and deserted part of the Opera – he was in no condition to resist me – and there I left him, below the fifth cellar, where no one ever comes and no one ever hears you. Then I went back to Christine. She was waiting for me."

Erik rose solemnly. Then he continued, trembling with emotion:

"She let me kiss her on the forehead. Oh, how good it is to kiss a person. You can't tell, you can't. But I! I! . . . My mother, my poor, unhappy mother would never let me kiss her. She used to run away and throw me my mask. Nor any other woman . . . ever, ever! You can understand, my happiness was so great, I cried. And I fell at her feet, crying. You're crying too, friend, and she also cried . . . the angel cried."

Erik sobbed aloud and the Persian himself could not restrain his tears in the presence of that masked man, who, with his shoulders shaking and his hands clutching at his chest, was moaning with pain and love by turns.

"I tore off my mask, she did not run away, and our tears mingled. We cried together. I have tasted all the happiness the world can offer."

And Erik fell into a chair, choking for breath.

"I am not going to die yet. Presently I shall, but let me cry for a while. Listen to this. . . . While I was at her feet, I heard her say: 'Poor, unhappy Erik.' *And she took my hand!* I had become no more, you know, than a poor dog, ready to die for her. I held in my hand a ring, a plain gold ring which I had given her . . . which she had lost, and which I had found again, a wedding ring, you know. I slipped it into her little hand and said, 'There. Take it. Take it for you and him. It shall be my wedding present, a present from your poor unhappy Erik. I know you love the boy. Don't cry any more.' She asked me, in a very soft voice, what I meant. Then I made her understand that, where she was concerned, I was only a poor dog, ready to die for her, and that she should marry the young man when she pleased, because she had cried with me and mingled her tears with mine!"

Erik's emotion was so great that he had to tell the Persian not to look at him, for he was choking and must take off his mask. The Persian went to the window and opened it. His heart was full of pity, but he took care to keep his eyes fixed on the trees in the Tuileries Gardens, lest he should see Erik's face.

"I went and released the young man," Erik continued, "and told him to come with me to Christine. They kissed before me in the Louis-Philippe room. Christine had my ring. I made Christine swear to come back, one night when I was dead, crossing the lake from the Rue-Scribe side, and bury me in the greatest secrecy with the gold ring, which she was to wear until that moment. I told her where she would find my body and what to do with it. Then Christine kissed me, for the first time, herself, here, on the forehead – don't look – on my forehead, mine, and they went off together. Christine had stopped crying. I alone cried. If Christine keeps her promise, she will come back soon."

Erik ceased speaking. The Persian asked him no questions. He was quite reassured as to the fate of Raoul de

Chagny and Christine Daaé: no one could have doubted the word of the weeping Erik that night.

Erik resumed his mask and collected his strength to leave the Persian. He told him that, when he felt his end to be close at hand, he would send him in gratitude for the kindness which the Persian had once shown him, the things which he held dearest in the world: all Christine Daaé's papers, letters which she had written to Raoul at the time of her kidnapping and left with Erik, together with a few objects belonging to her, such as a pair of gloves, a shoe buckle and two pocket handkerchiefs. In reply to the Persian's question, Erik told him that the young people, as soon as they found themselves free, had resolved to go and look for a priest in some lonely spot where they could hide their happiness and have a quiet wedding, for Raoul still mourned his brother. After that they thought they would leave the Opera which, no doubt, would carry on in much the same way, but without the mysteries and tragedies which had set little Giry and her friends all talking at once. Then perhaps they would disappear to the lakes of Norway, taking Mamma Valerius with them and Christine would sing in the mountains of the north just for them.

Lastly, Erik asked the Persian, as soon as he received the promised relics and papers, to inform the young couple of his death and to advertise it in the Paris newspapers.

That was all. The Persian saw Erik to the door of the flat and Darius helped him down to the street. A cab was waiting for him. Erik stepped in, and the Persian, who had gone to the window, heard him say to the driver:

"Go to the Opera."

And the cab drove off into the night.

The Persian had seen the poor, unhappy Erik for the last time.

Three weeks later, all the Paris newspapers published this advertisement:

Erik, the Phantom of the Opera, is dead.